**The Four-Blocks®
Literacy Model**

Self-Selected
Reading
The Four-Blocks® Way

by
Patricia M. Cunningham
Dorothy P. Hall
and
Linda B. Gambrell

Editors
Joey Bland
Tracy Soles

Cover Artist
Jennifer Collins

ISBN 0-88724-786-5

TABLE OF CONTENTS

A Peek into Classrooms
Doing Self-Selected Reading
the Four-Blocks® Way

The Self-Selected Reading Block looks different in different classrooms and at different grade levels. In Four-Blocks® classrooms, the Self-Selected Reading Block always includes the teacher reading aloud to the children from a wide range of literature and the children reading "on their own level" from self-selected books. The teacher holds conferences with children about their books, and opportunities are provided for children to share and respond to what is read.

 In this chapter, we will take an imaginary visit to a large elementary school, Fourblox Elementary. Linda Lerner is a reading resource teacher from Lotest Elementary. Lotest Elementary is in another school district in the same state and is trying to make some instructional changes, hoping to improve their students' reading and writing skills and test scores. Tom Baldman is the reading/language arts supervisor for the school district that includes Fourblox Elementary. Tom has helped all the schools in his district implement the Four-Blocks® framework. Tom's goal for the school system is to implement good, balanced reading instruction for the entire school district at all grade levels.

Today, Tom, a large bald man with a winning smile and a wonderful way with words, is doing a walk through Fourblox Elementary with Linda Lerner. Tom has taught kindergarten, first, and fifth grades. Having grown up in this school system, he knows the teachers and the administrators and is comfortable in the classrooms. Tom is helping Linda Lerner to look at each block and then use what she learns to support her teachers as they try to improve literacy instruction at Lotest Elementary. Tom and Linda's focus for the day is Self-Selected Reading.

First, Tom and Linda stop by the office to greet the new principal, Claire Leider. Claire was once a reading resource teacher who came to visit Fourblox, where her sister Melody was the music teacher. She spent the day watching Guided Reading at Fourblox and then later became the instructional leader at her own school. When the principal of Fourblox retired last year and the job was advertised, Claire, who had an administrator's certificate, decided to apply. Because she was so knowledgeable about Four-Blocks, she was the teachers' and the search committee's choice for this coveted position.

 "Here is today's schedule," says Claire, handing Tom a piece of paper with the times, teachers, grade levels, and classrooms listed. Tom and Linda will be spending the entire day at this large elementary school with only time for a quick lunch. This busy schedule puts a smile on both Tom and Linda's faces. They know they will be observing some of the best teachers and are sure to learn some new ideas from them that will help other teachers and students.

Here is what their schedule looks like:

Time	Teacher	Grade Level	Room No.
8:30-9:15	Deb Webb	Grade 2	Room 25
9:20-9:40	Bea Ginning	Kindergarten	Room 4
9:45-10:15	Cece Southern	Grade 1	Room 11
10:20-10:50	Laura Reading	Grade 2	Room 22
10:50-11:30	DeLinda DeLightful	Grade 3	Room 33
11:30-12:00	Randy Reid	Grade 4	Room 35
12:00-12:45	Lunch		
12:45-1:20	Joe Webman	Grade 1	Room 10
1:20- 1:55	Suzie Science	Grade 3	Room 30
2:00-2:30	Will Teachum	Grade 5	Room 40
2:30- 3:00	Diane DuRight	Kindergarten	Room 3

8:30–9:15   Mrs. Deb Webb   Grade 2   Room 25

Tom and Claire quietly walk into Deb's second-grade classroom. School has not yet started (it begins at 8:45 AM, but the children are allowed in the room at 8:30), and the students are busily, but quietly (for second graders!), roaming the room looking for books. Linda is taken aback by the sheer number of books in this classroom! "How did one teacher ever get so many books?" she wonders. She thought she had a lot of books in her own classroom, but nowhere near this number. The children are gathering their books for Self-Selected Reading, the first block on the agenda every day in Deb's classroom. There are two large book shelves against the wall in the back of the room that are full of books. There is a collection of books in blue plastic dishpans on a ledge in front of the windows. A quick glance shows names on the dishpans: Clifford, Dr. Seuss, Easy Chapter Books, Animal Books, Silly Stories, Gail Gibbons, Amelia Bedelia, etc. Many of Mrs. Webb's students have long bus rides to get to school, and she finds Self-Selected Reading a wonderful way to quiet down these students and begin school each day.

A few children already have their books and have begun reading at their desks. Deb is helping a child, Jackson, find one of the books that was read yesterday during the teacher read-aloud. Jackson not only wants to read this book, but it seems like only this book will do for him! After Deb finds the book, she helps Jackson find a few "just right" books and an insect book (which is her theme at this time). Then, she moves on to help another child who is pondering over her choices from the dishpan marked "Easy Chapter Books."

To open the Self-Selected Reading Block, Deb Webb gathers the children close to her. They sit at her feet as cozily as possible in a classroom. Tom had told Linda, before they entered the classroom, that Deb tries to imitate the setting of bedtime stories and routines for those who were not fortunate enough to have someone to read to them at home. Tom also explained that Deb chooses three different books for her daily teacher read-aloud—a chapter book, a nonfiction book related to the theme the class is studying, and an "everyone book." She does not call the "everyone" books "easy" books, but they are short, simple, predictable pattern books that everyone in her second-grade class can read. Tom explained that the struggling readers are willing to read books that the teacher reads first, and Deb reads and "blesses" an "everyone book" every day!

Mrs. Webb begins the teacher read-aloud portion of Self-Selected Reading with a chapter book. It is evident that she has read this book before because there are sticky notes attached to some of the pages of the book, and on these sticky notes, she has written down her thoughts. Today, Deb is reading the third chapter of *Lions at Lunchtime (Magic Tree House 11)* by Mary Pope Osborne. As Deb reads, she is modeling the think-aloud procedure she has taught her class to use during Guided Reading. Deb has read chapters one and two, and the class discusses the story so far.

> "In the first chapter, we met a brother and sister, Jack and Annie, who followed a tiny deer into the woods and found a magic tree house. We wondered what they would find in the woods. We thought maybe a tree house because that is in the name of the book, and we were right! My son has a tree house, but not like this one! In this tree house, Jack and Annie are given a book called *The Plains of Africa* by Morgan le Fay. What does Annie say when she looks at the book?"

Ashleigh answers, "Annie says, 'I wish we could go there.'"

> "Have you ever said that? I have! Usually nothing happens, but not so for Jack and Annie. Next thing they knew, they were on their way, and the second chapter finds them in Africa watching the animals."

After reading the title of chapter three, "Disaster," Deb stops to ask the class what they think is going to happen in this chapter.

"Something bad!" says a little boy on the front row. "Wonder what?" asks the girl sitting next to him.

> "Let's read to find out what the disaster is in this chapter."

The children perk up as they learn how zebras, wildebeests, and gazelles are connected. The chapter ends with Jack not being able to find Annie.

> "Will Jack find Annie?" Deb asks. "I hope we find that out when we read tomorrow!"

Deb, like many of the students, seems enchanted by the *Magic Tree House* stories and helps her students join the make-believe journey with the two characters in the book. She tells them what she likes about reading: "Books can take you anywhere, even to faraway Africa!"

Next, Deb shares a few pages of a nonfiction book. The class is studying about insects, so she reads *Insects* by Robin Bernard. The pictures are beautiful, and the simple explanations make this book appealing to many school-age children. Deb begins the book, " The world is full of creepy crawly things. But not all of them are insects." She does not read the whole book, just a few pages and talks about the things she learns on each page. She tells the class that she will put the book in the insect book tub for those who want to read more about insects. Tom makes a mental note of this book and writes down the title and author. He wants to add *Insects* to his personal collection of children's books.

Mrs. Webb closes the read-aloud time with her "everyone book." She reads *Zoo Animals* by Mary E. Pearson.

> "I chose this book for my 'everyone read' because it is about some African animals we find in the zoo. It begins like this, 'A monkey swings.... A lion climbs.... A giraffe runs....'"

Linda Lerner notes that Mrs. Webb talks about the pictures, reads with expression, and looks as if she is enjoying the book. When Deb finishes, she asks Jackson if he would like this book to add to those on his desk. He eagerly grabs for it. He is one of those children who love to reread stories they have just heard. Next, Mrs. Webb looks into the basket where there are a few more copies of the book, and she shares the name of another book by the same author, *Zoo Animal Surprise*. She tells the class that this book does not have real pictures; it is a make-believe story about zoo animals.

After Deb Webb reads from the chapter book, the informational book, and the "everyone book," the children return to their seats where the 5-8 books they chose are on their desks waiting for them. Deb watches as they settle in with their chosen books. She is ready to help anyone who needs it, but no one seems to need extra help today. Deb then sits down with Jackson and listens to him read his book. She notices that he makes two mistakes when decoding, but he self-corrects both of them and then glances over at her to make sure she noticed that he knew what to do when it "didn't sound right." When Jackson is finished reading, she praises him for his self-corrections. "O-o-oh, what a good reader you are!" Next, Jackson begins a picture walk through the insect book, looking at the pictures and talking about the things he observes in them. Deb decides that Jackson is not only learning to read in second grade; he is also learning about the themes they are studying. He has come a long way since September.

Deb moves on to another desk nearby and conferences with Ashleigh, then Alex, and finally David. Linda notes to herself: four different children, four different reading levels, four different book choices, and four children nudged forward in their literacy learning in just 20 minutes!

9:20-9:40   **Miss Bea Ginning**   **Kindergarten**   **Room 4**

As they walk down the hall and around the corner to a kindergarten class, Tom shares with Linda that Bea Ginning is just about to finish her first full year of teaching. Tom tells Linda that Bea loves teaching Building Blocks™, the Four-Blocks kindergarten model. He explains, "For a first-year teacher, she knows the model well, having learned it in college and having student-taught with a wonderful Building Blocks teacher. Her cooperating teacher was pregnant at the time and chose to stay home with her new baby boy. Now Bea is the 'real' teacher and a wonderful one."

Tom and Linda enter the kindergarten class and slip quietly into the back of the room. The children are gathered in a "big group" on a colorful carpet, with Bea sitting in a rocking chair and the children sitting in four small rows in front of her. The calendar is to the left of the big group and can be seen by all. Tom and Linda can see that Bea has already done the calendar and weather activities because the sentences are in the pocket chart. They also see that Bea has written a morning message, and as they read the second line, they find out that the news for the day is, "Two visitors are coming to our classroom today." They can see the big book she will use later for Guided Reading sitting nearby. The title of the book is *A Family Is Special* by Darwin Walton. It is an informational book (nonfiction) with photographs of families. (Tom and Linda cannot see the text, but the book is predictable by pictures and print, with sentences that begin, "A family can....") Tom and Linda also see a predictable chart that has been written recently about families. The predictable part of the chart is, "A family can...." The writing center has family words for the class's family picture dictionary (father, mother, sister, brother, baby, grandmother, grandfather, cousin). The home center has clothes for "mother" and "father" to wear and a baby doll for the family to care for. It's easy to see that almost everything in this classroom is tied into the theme they are studying—families.

Now Bea is ready to read the first read-aloud book of the day to the class. She talks about the items on the cover— the name of the book, the author, the illustrator, and the picture. "What do you think this book is about?" she asks. From the cover, the class decides that it is about a family. Tom and Linda also know that it is a story (fiction) by the illustrations. Ms. Ginning begins to read, "Jessie was worried and sad. She couldn't find her bear anywhere." Bea continues reading until, at the end, Jessie finds her bear in the doghouse with the new puppy, who is also part of this family!

Right after the read-aloud that ends "big group," Bea lets the children spend a few minutes reading. They started earlier in the year with five minutes. Now, they are up to seven minutes. The children sit at their tables and select books from the purple plastic crates at each table. There are approximately 25 books in each crate. Tom and Linda notice that the crates are full of wonderful books for kindergarten students, and include familiar and favorite books that Bea has read to the class, like *The Very Hungry Caterpillar* and *A House for Hermit Crab* by Eric Carle and *Swimmy* by Leo Leonni. All the children can now "retell" these stories because Bea has taken a few minutes to model this procedure each day. There are also easy-leveled readers in the baskets because many of the children can "really read" these books. Then, there are books from themes and subjects they have studied this year in kindergarten that all the children can now "picture read." Bea reminds the class of the three ways they read in kindergarten (retell the story, picture read, or really read), and then dismisses the tables by their colors, "The blue group can go back to their table and read; red group next; green group go quietly back on tiptoes; purple group tiptoe next; and the last group is yellow. Let's see if you can walk, then read just as quietly as the other tables."

Bea monitors her little ones and sees that they are choosing their books quietly, just like she taught them. She walks over to Corey because she knows he always seems to need her to start his picture reading. Once he is "on task," Bea sits down with the green table; it is their turn for the teacher today. Ryan is the first student at the green table to read to her. He is an average student, but reading easy-leveled readers fluently. He does a wonderful retelling of the story *Grandpa, Grandpa* by Joy Cowley and can turn to and talk about his favorite part of the book. Bea listens to her students read, coaches them if needed, and briefly discusses each book with them. She has a range of readers at each table and accepts the way they read or pretend read their books. (This is also true of the other tables she will listen to and conference with later in the week.) Bea "ooohs" and "aahs" over how well they are reading. The children seem as happy and upbeat as their first-year teacher.

Linda comments, "I never seem to have students like this come to my first-grade class." Tom and Linda tiptoe out of the classroom, just like these kindergarten students did on the way back to their seats. Once they are outside the door, Tom says, "Aren't Building Blocks classrooms wonderful? Bea's hard work this year really shows. Those youngsters are ready for first grade." Linda couldn't agree more. As they walk down the hall, Linda and Tom talk about what Bea did to get to this point with her students.

9:45-10:15   Mrs. Cece Southern   Grade 1   Room 11

Cece is finishing up her Guided Reading Block as the two visitors reach her classroom. The children are gathered in front of the room, and Cece stands and does the "macarena" with her class to help them move, stretch, and get the "wiggles" out before she begins her read-aloud. As the students sit down, Cece lifts the book she will begin to read to them today from the chalk ledge. With both hands, she holds the book close to her heart. "Today, I am going to read one of my favorite books to you. It is a chapter book, but it does not have too many chapters, and it's not too long. In fact, I think it is just right for first-graders. It is about a funny girl name Junie B. Jones." Mrs. Southern then turns the book around, shows the class the cover, points with her finger to the name of the book, *Junie B. Jones Is a Party Animal,* and the author's name, Barbara Park. Cece then shows the students what the illustrator thinks Junie B. Jones looks like. "Junie B. Jones is younger than you. She is in kindergarten in this book. But is she ever funny! I remember last year, when I had a student that used to make me laugh just like Junie B. Jones does when I read this book. Listen as I read the first chapter, and see if you think Junie B. Jones is funny."

Cece begins to read the first chapter of this easy chapter book. There is no doubt that she has the full attention of the class. After reading, they discuss what Junie does and says that makes her so funny and enjoyable.

Next, as the book baskets are passed out by the table leaders, Cece explains that they will find not only their favorite and familiar picture books in the baskets, but a few easy chapter books, including some *Junie B. Jones* books! She reminds the students that they have to find a book they can read and how they want something "just right." She also reminds them to read quietly and use the "phonics phone" if they need to. Tom and Linda notice that there are a few of these in each basket. (A phonics phone is actually a piece of plastic pipe called a PVC valve and can be bought at any of the large home improvement or hardware stores.) A few children who cannot read silently find these PVC "phones" and begin reading into them. The PVC pipe allows the children to hear themselves, even when they are whispering, and this keeps the room quieter.

Cece then sits at a table on one side of the room and calls children over to conference with her, one by one. The children listed under Wednesday on her list for Self-Selected Reading Conferences, which is posted on the wall behind her, are called. The children know that they should bring with them a favorite book they have read since their last conference with Mrs. Southern. They also know to place a sticky note on the page or pages they want to read before they come. They are prepared to retell the story or talk about their favorite part. The children love this time every week, as they share special books with their special teacher.

Tom remarks to Mrs. Southern on his way out that he remembers when first-graders at this school, for the most part, could not and did not read chapter books in first grade. Cece says she remembers that, too, and adds, "We are doing more reading now. We certainly have more books in our classroom! But, for the children and the teachers, what's best is that we have the time to read what we want, and we are having more fun!"

10:20 – 10:50   Mrs. Laura Reading   Grade 2   Room 22

As Tom and Linda enter this classroom, Laura Reading is seated in a comfortable chair with her students at her feet. Nearby, there is an aquarium with several interesting fish swimming back and forth. Laura is holding a book about fish titled, *What's It Like To Be a Fish?* written by Wendy Pfeffer and illustrated by Holly Keller.

"Today, I have chosen a book about fish to read to you. I thought this would be really interesting since we have a new aquarium in our room, and I have been asked so many questions about fish lately. Let's see if this book will answer any of your questions."

Laura begins to read, holding the book so the children can see it. "Fish live in water—in lakes, ponds, aquariums, and even plastic bags. Your pet goldfish can live in a bowl. You can watch the golden fish slip over and under the castle." At this point, several pairs of eyes look at the aquarium in the classroom to see if they have a castle (no) or water plants (yes). Laura continues, "The next page is about the fish's body."

Laura points to each part of the fish in the picture as she reads its name. Some children try to find these parts on the real fish swimming in their tank. Laura continues to read, page by page, commenting on how the pictures in this book help us to understand what the author is telling us about fish.

"What questions did this book help answer?" Laura asks. Several hands go up. When Bobby is called upon, he says he learned that fish need only a pinch of food—so they are feeding their fish correctly. Kathy says she learned why they have a thermometer in their aquarium—fish need the water to be about 72 degrees.

Next, Mrs. Reading reads a chapter of *Arthur Makes the Team* by Marc Brown. Because it's spring and many of her second-graders are planning to play on little league teams, she thought this book might make one or two of them feel better. They, too, may act like klutzes at times and are worried they won't be able to play as well as their friends. The children listen as Laura reads this short chapter, and when she finishes, they are ready to relate the text to self—just like they have learned to do in Guided Reading. "I felt just like Arthur when I first started practicing. I thought I would miss the ball, and sometimes I did!" said Bobby.

For their independent reading of self-selected books, Laura lets her class sit anywhere they want. She dismisses the back row to "sit where they want." The youngsters head for their favorite places: one moves to the teacher's chair, several go to the book nook to sit on an old sofa she has brought to school, others head for the corners of the class and plop down on pillows where they can "curl up with a good book." One row at a time is dismissed for the students to find their "own space," and they do. It is evident that Laura has trained them well, and they know  that as long as they follow the rules, they have the freedom to sit where they want. Laura begins roaming around the room, getting a few students on task and redirecting a few others to use their "whisper voices." Then, she looks at her reading conference list for the day and joins those students in their special places. As Laura talks to her students about their books, she helps them make connections to the text if they are not already doing so.

Tom says to Linda, "That's Laura, always teaching a strategy in Guided Reading and then making sure the kids use it with the books they choose during Self-Selected Reading." He glances at the clock and realizes that another 30 minutes has flown by, and they need to be heading down the hall to the next classroom on their list.

10:50 -11:30   Mrs. DeLinda DeLightful   Grade 3   Room 33

As Tom and Linda enter this classroom, they are greeted by someone they both know—DeLinda DeLightful. "This is the block I look most forward to each day; we have so much fun!" she tells her visitors. The children are entering the room now also, having just returned from a bathroom break. Sitting in a big, red, comfortable chair in front of her students, DeLinda begins, "I am so excited today to share...." Before she can finish her sentence, her third-graders chime in to finish the familiar sentence, "your favorite new book!" The children know that Mrs. DeLightful has many, many favorite books and is always finding "a favorite new book." She shows them the new book, *The Brand New Kid* by Katie Couric. The class is amazed; they did not know that this television personality was also a writer of children's books. DeLinda explains that this is the first book Katie Couric has written. "See if you like it," she says, as she begins reading from this new picture book. It is evident that DeLinda likes the drama of reading this book to her class and keeping their interest from page to page. She has the children laughing on some pages and almost crying on others. Do they like it? "YES!" Do they think Katie should write another? "YES!"

Next, DeLinda reads from an old favorite, *Miles of Smiles: Kids Pick the Funniest Poems* by Bruce Lansky. Just as she kept their interest page to page when reading Katie's book, she now has the students' undivided attention poem after poem. DeLinda reads several poems, which vary in length and subject, from this thick collection of poetry. She notices how much everyone is enjoying the poems, so she makes a mental note to look harder for more poetry books for her third-grade students. It is evident from her class that chapter books are important in third grade, but they are not the only reading material that is appealing. After each poem, the class discusses what they liked or thought about the poems.

Then, DeLinda sends the class back to their seats. When the children are all quietly at their seats and tubs full of books are on certain desks, DeLinda says, "I wonder what tub these books will go in today?" The students then get very still, hoping their good behavior will determine the tub. DeLinda walks quietly around the room and drops the two books in two different tubs, much to the delight of the students sitting near those two spots.

A look in the tubs shows a variety of books available: picture books, easy chapter books, harder chapter books, poetry books, informational books, science books, joke books, laminated *Weekly Readers*, classroom-published books, even some children's cookbooks. In each tub there are also bookmarks so that when reading a book they will need again the next day, the students can put a bookmark inside. If a book has a bookmark with a name showing, then the class knows only that student can read it.

As the students get their books for Self-Selected Reading and begin to read, Mrs. DeLightful sits at her "conference" table. As in the other classes, the children in this class are assigned to a certain day of the week to conference with the teacher, and they know to be ready on that day. Robbie is first today, and he conferences about a nonfiction book he has read. DeLinda asks, " Was it too hard, was it just right, or was it too easy?" Robbie says honestly, "Oh, it was too hard, but I love looking at the graphs and charts. I can read most of the words under them." Then, he shares some facts he learned by reading this book. DeLinda ends the conference by thanking Robbie for sharing his book with her, "I learned some new facts that I didn't know before!" (Tom tells Linda Lerner that Robbie is exactly why we should not limit what children read to just books on their reading level.) DeLinda continues her conferences, making each one a special time for the students, not an assessment time.

DeLinda ends her conferences and announces that it is time for "Chair Chat." The children know how to share because they have watched the book reviews at the end of "Reading Rainbow" tapes to learn how to do a book talk. They know they will have two minutes, and a timer will be used to keep them to that limit. The big comfy, red chair that was previously the teacher's chair is now the "chat chair," and beside it is the "Chair Chat Chart." Each child who had a conference with the teacher today now gets a chance to share with the class. They follow the order of the chart, telling about their book—its genre, their favorite part, etc. The children get to speak into a karaoke microphone. It is turned up for the quiet children, and all the way down for those who could be heard "a mile down the road." After each child shares her book, the others get to ask a question. Before the first person shares each day, Mrs. DeLightful reminds the students to, "Ask a thinking question, not a parrot question." A parrot question, she explains, is one that is always asked. When students put a lot of thinking into their questions, DeLinda never fails to remark, "What a great thinking question that was!" Since it is Wednesday, DeLinda reminds the class that it is "Choice Night"—they can take a book of their choice home from the book buckets, as long as they remember to return it the next day. The children love to read and share favorite books from Self-Selected Reading with their parents. Tom and Linda realize that it is time to leave this "delightful" teacher and visit the next name on their agenda. Time flies when you are having fun, hearing good stories and seeing good teaching!

11:30-12:00   Mr. Randy Reid   Grade 4   Room 35

Randy Reid is reading to his fourth-grade class as Tom and Linda enter this final room before lunch. They notice the book Randy is reading, a new favorite of many elementary students, *The Adventures of Captain Underpants* by Dav Pilkey. In the book, two fourth-graders, George and Harold, create the greatest superhero of their elementary school, Captain Underpants. The class, especially the boys, seem to enjoy this outrageously funny, action-packed, yet easy-to-read chapter book. It is also written on a reading level that most students in the room can read. Mr. Reid is sitting in the front of his class with his students huddled close so that they not only hear the story, but can see the pictures also. Some pages are written like a comic strip, and many of the pages have pictures that have to be seen and enjoyed, so sitting close to the reader is a must. The chapters are short (perfect for his reluctant readers), so Randy reads two chapters in just over five minutes. Next, the children return to their seats and read. Most of these fourth-graders are reading chapter books, many of them reading the thin, easy-to-read type that Randy has collected in the last few years. Randy has also found that fourth-graders like to read and learn facts. Some of the children are reading picture books about a state of their choice. The fourth-graders study their own state at Fourblox Elementary, and Randy has a collection of books about all 50 states that contain "the facts" in an interesting format. Others students like books on science subjects: the solar system, electricity, snakes, animals, tornadoes, etc. Randy has shelves of books on the side of his room with a large variety of books (fiction, information, and reference materials). The children who want their books from yesterday go to the "reserve" shelf, and those who need a new book are browsing. Randy helps a few make wise choices; he knows a good choice may lead to several days of reading material. Mr. Reid also lets children bring books from home, so some children are seen pulling books out of their desks or book bags and reading for the next 20 minutes.

Randy has a list of students to conference with. He goes to each student's desk to conference. When all students on the list have had a conference, he begins again. During the last 5 minutes of class each day, Randy lets the students "pair and share." They pair with someone nearby and share what they are reading about, what they learned from a book, or what happened in the book/chapter they read today. Randy "spies on" the students during this time, which means he listens to several pairs who are sharing. Linda Lerner and Tom Baldman realize another 30 minutes have gone by, and it is time for them to head to the next thing on their schedule—lunch!

12:00 – 12:45 Lunch

Tom and Linda join a class and go through the lunch line, choosing from the menu along with the students. Next, they look for a quiet corner in the huge school cafeteria. Hurrying into the room, the principal, Claire Leider, invites them down the hall to her office where they can sit at a small, quiet, table. They realize that they have only 35 minutes to eat and talk—no leisurely lunches in large (or small) elementary schools. Both have so much to say about all they have observed and what they want to remember to share with teachers at workshops in the future. "Every time I watch a good Four-Blocks teacher, I learn something new," says Linda. "I've noticed that, too," says Tom.

12:45 -1:20   Mr. Joe Webman   Grade 1   Room 10

Joe Webman is the first teacher they visit after lunch. Ms. Lerner and Mr. Baldman enter the classroom as the eager first-graders return from recess. One by one, the children gather in front of Mr. Webman, who is sitting on a tall stool. He takes out Jack Prelutsky's *The New Kid on the Block*, as pleas for the reading of "Homework, Oh Homework" abound. Instead, the teacher reads two humorous selections. He then turns to a well-worn page and starts to read, "Homework, Oh Homework, I hate you, You stink …." and the children happily join in. The poem is obviously one of their favorites.

Finally, Mr. Webman brings out the book *My Puppy Is Born* by Joanna Cole. One child excitedly comments about the cute little puppy on the cover. Another student eagerly announces that his dog is going to have puppies very soon. Margaret Miller's photographs captivate the students as the text about a Norfolk terrier pup's first six weeks of life is read. When the selection is completed, Mr. Webman is bombarded with questions and comments. He listens to some, and then announces that soon a basket of books about animals and their babies will be placed in one of the reading corners.

Mr. Webman comments that the story of the puppy reminds him of a book that was read earlier in the year. The boys and girls start shouting out titles as the teacher presents the next book to be read. The whole class shouts their approval when they see *Biscuit* by Alyssa Satin Capucilli in the teacher's hand. As Joe reads the story, the children add the familiar "Woof! Woof!" sounds at the appropriate places.

With a basket of books in hand, Mr. Webman announces to the class that a new basket of dog books is going to be placed in one of the reading corners. First, he pulls out several *Biscuit* titles that are available, followed by some *Clifford* books by Norman Bridwell, and several of the *Harry the Dirty Dog* titles by Gene Zion. The children are familiar with these books and look eager to start reading. The teacher then begins to read a new selection, *Martha Speaks* by Susan Meddaugh. He reads about how the dog Martha eats a bowl of alphabet soup and the letters go to her brain instead of her stomach. When he reaches this point in the story, he stops and shuts the book. As he puts the book back in the basket, the children plead with him to complete the book. Mr. Webman simply encourages the students to read the book for themselves.

The children are then dismissed. They move to the assigned reading corner, select a book, and move away and begin to read. Soon Mr. Webman is moving among the six reading corners, making positive comments. Once the children are settled, he begins spending a few minutes individually with five pre-selected students. Mrs. Lerner listens as each child reads from a book of his choice while the teacher coaches and praises the student's reading.

After about 15 minutes, the timer goes off, indicating that the Self-Selected Reading Block is over. The students quickly grab a book, return to their seats, fill out a book checkout form, and place the book in a resealable plastic bag. As Mrs. Lerner and Mr. Baldman get up to leave, Mr. Webman explains that the books in the plastic bags will go home that night to be read. The books will be returned the following day.

> "Read to your parents or your grandparents, read to your pets or your stuffed animals, read to yourself, just as long as you read tonight!"

1:20-1:55   Miss Suzie Science   Grade 3   Room 30

Tom and Linda's next visit is to another third-grade classroom, but this room looks more like a science lab. There are plants growing everywhere. There is a rabbit in one cage, two gerbils in another cage, and some fish in an aquarium. There are "special spots" to explore with magnets, magnifying glasses, and a microscope. There is also a writing center with a computer, an old typewriter, journals, writing/note paper (This is one classroom where note writing is OK!), and places to explore other science topics.

Suzie is holding one of the *Magic School Bus* books in her hand. The children wonder which one. When all the children are gathered on the side of the room in the "special spot" just right for the whole class, Suzie sits on a small stool with wheels (since she often slides here or there to show something or point) and tells the class that when they were studying the solar system they read a big book during Guided Reading called *The Magic School Bus: Lost in the Solar System* by Joanna Cole. At that time, they learned there were three kinds of text in these *Magic School Bus* books: fiction (the story), cartoons (the word balloons), and information (writing and pictures on notebook paper on the side of the page). The book she has chosen for today has to do with what they will be studying next in third grade—the water cycle. Fourblox Elementary is located in a state that has a "standard course of study" in every subject, at every grade level. Suzie finds the science objectives for third grade are easy to teach when you integrate them into all four blocks of instruction. During the Self-Selected Reading Block today, she reads a book that introduces her students to the water cycle, *The Magic School Bus: At the Water Works* by Joanna Cole. The students listen intently to the story. The children smile as they notice the resemblance between their teacher, Suzie Science, and the teacher in this book, Miss Frizell. Both teachers like wearing crazy clothes with animals, plants, or creatures on them. The class knows that their upcoming field trip will not be nearly as exciting as the field trip they are reading about, but they know that they will learn a lot about the water cycle from Miss Science before and after the trip. They know to take notebooks and make notes just as the students in the book do. The notes will become a written report of the field trip. The students listen as Suzie Science reads and talks; they know this is a preview of things to come. She also compares this field trip to what they will see at the local water works. "Bring your bathing suits," Suzie Science jokes, "We might just dive right in like these students!"

Once Suzie finishes the book, she gives a short book talk on each of the new titles she has added to the purple plastic crates at the side of the room. Some students who are reading novels are even tempted to try one of these books today. "She could sell anyone any book," says one student. "She's sold me on one of those books!" says another as he heads to the crates. As Suzie dismisses the children, some of them take a purple plastic crate and others follow. The children move quietly to their desks. The crates are placed at special spots so they will not wander around the room for a book; books are always close by!

The purple plastic crates are filled with a wide variety of books because Suzie knows she has a wide range of readers in her third-grade class. Favorite picture books, favorite chapter books, easy-to-read chapter books, books on recent science and social studies topics, and now books about the water cycle are only a few of the choices. Suzie knows that third-graders read about anything. She also knows that having time to work with her struggling readers during the Self-Selected Reading Block is important. Every day, she has the name of one struggling student on her list, and that student gets the first and longest of her one-on-one conferences during Self-Selected Reading. Miss Science also conferences with one or two of her super readers each day. She knows that these students are far ahead of the third-grade level and need to be challenged. She loves her chats with her students, especially if they are reading about science subjects!

2:00-2:30   Mr. Will Teachum   Grade 5   Room 40

Will is a wonderful teacher, and his students both like and respect him. He expects a lot from his fifth-graders, but they like him so much they will do anything and not complain. He is a wonderful math, writing, science, social studies, and health teacher. Name any subject at the intermediate level, and Will can teach it. He is also a computer whiz, just like Joe Webman, his friend down the hall. As Tom and Linda enter the room, Will is sitting at his desk reading a "new" favorite, *Because of Winn-Dixie* by Kate DiCamillo. Tom smiles when he sees that this book has a silver Newbery Honor Book seal on the front cover. Will likes for his students to read "good literature," so he is always sharing Newbery winners and Honor Books with his class. Will also finds that many of these are realistic fiction, and they give him a chance to bring up topics that ten-year-olds think (and worry!) about. This story is no exception.

As Linda listens to Will's review, she finds out that India Opal Buloni lives with her dad, who is a preacher in Florida. Opal's mother left them when Opal was three, and she misses her mother. Winn-Dixie is the name of a dog this ten-year-old meets and adopts while at the supermarket. Opal tells this dog how she feels about everything. Today's two chapters are short and about the librarian, Miss Franny Block, who tells Opal about her grandfather. He fought in the Civil War and started a candy factory once he returned home and found out he was the only one left alive in his family. Miss Block then goes to her desk and gets some Litmus Lozenger and shares her grandfather's candy with Opal, Winn-Dixie, and another child who has stopped to listen. This book is full of "feelings," and the children get to tell how they would feel if that happened to them.

After reading today's two chapters, the students get their book boxes from some shelves nearby and begin to read. In their book boxes, they have their current book, the next book they plan to read, a book that interests them about something they are studying, and a newspaper or magazine. Mr. Teachum begins to call students up for their weekly conference, and the students look pleased to go and share their books with him. When a student is reading a Newbery winner, you can tell that Will is very pleased. He introduces children to all the genres, but the children know Newbery books are his favorites, so many choose them. At first, his students chose those books so they could please their teacher, but after reading two or three award-winning books, the students now choose the books because they like them!

2:30-3:00   Mrs. Diane DuRight   Kindergarten   Room 3

Last year, Diane was a third-grade teacher, but when a vacancy arose this year, she chose to teach kindergarten. Everyone was surprised because Diane was such a great third-grade teacher. Diane wanted to move down and help children learn to read sooner (and besides, there are NO tests in kindergarten!). Diane is reading *Gingerbread Boy* stories to her students this week, and *Gingerbread Baby* by Jan Brett is the one she has chosen for today. The students can't wait to hear the story and compare it to the two other stories that have been read. Diane begins to read to the class, discussing the beautiful illustrations as she reads. She stops and talks, and then reads some more. She compares this book with the two others books she has read to them. The students think this is their favorite version so far. Then, Diane dismisses her students to their tables. Her kindergarten students read for a short while at their desks while Diane circulates around the room, encouraging and coaching. The children do their self-selected reading from books that are stored in large, clear, plastic tubs; one tub has been set on each table at this time. The children have increased their reading time to 10 minutes by this point in the year. When the kitchen timer goes off, they beg for more time. "Maybe 12 minutes next week!" Diane says. She loves the Building Blocks™ activities, and she knows that she is developing a love of reading and real reading behaviors while doing these activities. Diane DuRight is doing it right in kindergarten, just as she did when teaching third grade.

The day is almost over, and Tom Baldman and Linda Lerner realize that their visit to Fourblox Elementary School has come to an end. They have learned a lot from watching good teachers, and Linda is anxious to pick up a few books she does not have in her collection of children's books. "I'm off to the mall to buy two books I just have to have after hearing portions of them today. There's a big sale at the bookstore." She might have to stop by some other stores; shopping is another favorite activity of hers—after reading, of course!

2

THE FOUR-BLOCKS® FRAMEWORK

In the previous chapter, you observed classrooms at all different grade levels during their Self-Selected Reading Block. Self-Selected Reading is one of the four blocks of instructional time which, along with the Guided Reading, Writing, and Working with Words blocks, make up the Four-Blocks® framework. In this chapter, we will share with you:

- An overview of the Four-Blocks® framework.
- An overview of the other three blocks—Guided Reading, Writing, and Working with Words, including their goals and how they are multilevel.
- An overview of Self-Selected Reading.
- The role of Self-Selected Reading in the Building Blocks™ framework for kindergarten and the Big Blocks™ framework for upper grades.
- Some connections we make between Self-Selected Reading, the other blocks, and other curriculum areas.

How and Why the Four-Blocks® Framework Was Developed

The Four-Blocks® framework was developed by teachers who believed that to be successful in teaching ALL children to read and write, we were going to have to do it ALL! "Doing it all" means incorporating on a daily basis the different approaches to reading. The four blocks—Self-Selected Reading, Guided Reading, Writing, and Working with Words—represent four different approaches to teaching children to read. Daily instruction in all four blocks provides numerous and varied opportunities for all children to learn to read and write. Doing all four blocks acknowledges that children do not all learn in the same way and provides substantial instruction to support whatever learning personality a child has. The other big difference between children—their different literacy levels—is acknowledged by using a variety of activities to make each block as multilevel as possible, providing additional support for children who struggle and additional challenges for children who catch on quickly.

The Four-Blocks® framework began in 1989-90 in one first-grade classroom (Cunningham, Hall & Defee, 1991; Cunningham, Hall & Defee, 1998). In the 1990-91 school year, 16 first-grade teachers in four schools used the framework, making modifications to suit a variety of different school populations, including a Title 1 school (Hall, Prevatte & Cunningham, 1995). Since 1991, the framework has been used in numerous first-, second- and third-grade classrooms where many children still struggle with reading and writing.

(For more information about the Four-Blocks® framework, see *The Teacher's Guide to the Four-Blocks®* by Cunningham, Hall & Sigmon, 1999; *The Four Blocks: A Framework for Reading and Writing in Classrooms That Work*, a videotape by Cunningham and Hall, 1999; the "Four Blocks Column" by Cheryl Sigmon at *www.teachers.net* and the 4-Blocks Mailrings at *teachers.net* and *www.readinglady.com*.)

The Four-Blocks® framework has many variations, but there are two basic principles which must be followed if reading and writing instruction can truly be called Four Blocks. First, because it is believed (and research supports the idea) that children learn to read in different ways, each block gets 30-40 minutes of instruction each and every day. Providing enough and equal time to each block assures that children are given the same opportunity to become literate, regardless of which approach is most compatible with their individual learning personalities. The second basic principle is that while children are not put in fixed ability groups, the instruction is made as multilevel as possible so that average, struggling, and excelling students all learn to read and write at the highest possible level. Doing the four blocks every day and giving them approximately equal time is a simple matter of making a schedule and sticking to it. Making the instruction in each block as multilevel as possible is more complex, but it can be done. You will see many examples of this throughout this book.

Guided Reading, Writing, and Working with Words

Guided Reading

Guided Reading lessons usually have a before-reading phase, a during-reading phase, and an after-reading phase. Depending on the text being read, the comprehension strategies being taught, and the reading levels of the children, we use a great variety of before-, during-, and after-reading variations. Before children read, we help them build and access prior knowledge, make connections to personal experiences, develop vocabulary essential for comprehension, make predictions, and set purposes for their reading. After reading, we help children connect new knowledge to what they knew before, follow up predictions, and discuss what we learned and how we are becoming better readers by using our reading strategies.

In Four-Blocks classrooms, children read the selections in all different kinds of formats. On some days, the whole class reads together, and the teacher uses shared reading, choral reading, echo reading, or Everyone Read To... (ERT...) to encourage everyone's active participation. On other days, the children may read the selection in partners, playschool groups, book club groups, or think-aloud groups. Sometimes, teachers pull small coaching groups and read a selection with them while the other children read the selection in partners or individually.

The goals of the Guided Reading Block are:
- To teach comprehension skills and strategies.
- To develop background knowledge, meaning vocabulary, and oral language.
- To teach children how to read all types of literature.
- To provide as much instructional-level reading as possible.
- To maintain the motivation and self-confidence of struggling readers.

Guided Reading is the hardest block to make multilevel. Any selection is going to be too hard for some children and too easy for others. Here are some of the most common ways to make Guided Reading multilevel:

- Guided Reading time is not spent only in grade-level material. Rather, teachers alternate selections—one at the average reading level of the class and one easier.

- In book club groups, select four books tied together in some way. In selecting these books, include one that is a little easier than average and one that is a little harder.

- Reread each selection—or parts of longer selections—several times, each time for a different purpose in a different format. Rereading enables children who couldn't read it fluently the first time to achieve fluent reading by the last reading.

- Children who need help are not left to read by themselves, but are supported in a variety of ways. Most teachers use reading partners and playschool groups and teach children how to coach each other.

- On some days, some children read the selection by themselves and others read with partners while the teacher meets with a small group. These small coaching groups change regularly and do not include only the low readers.

- Some teachers schedule their Guided Reading time when they have "help" coming. Guided Reading can be more multilevel if you have more adults working with coaching groups or circulating and providing support to partners or groups.

- Provide some extra easy-reading time for children whose reading level is well below even the easier selections read. Some teachers meet with children individually or in small groups while the rest of the children are engaged in center or other activities. Include some good reading models in your "Fun Reading Club" or "After Lunch Bunch." The most struggling readers are included more often. These small group or individual easy-reading sessions are always in addition to—not substituted for—the instruction included during the Four-Blocks.

- When available, coordinate with early intervention teachers and/or tutors to provide guided reading instruction on appropriate levels for the children with whom they work.

- Spread out your struggling readers across the days for Self-Selected Reading conferences. Conference first with them each day, giving them a little extra time and making sure they select books they will enjoy and can read.

One way or another, we try to make sure that children are getting the support they need, including some coaching each week, as they read material at their instructional level.

(Detailed descriptions of before- and after-reading activities and during-reading formats can be found in *Guided Reading the Four-Blocks® Way* by Cunningham, Hall, and Cunningham, 2000.)

Writing
The Writing Block includes both self-selected writing, in which children choose their topics, and focused writing in which children learn how to write particular forms and on particular topics. Children are taught to use process writing to improve their first drafts, so they don't have to think of

everything at one time. Process writing is carried out in "Writers' Workshop" fashion (Graves, 1995; Routman, 1995; Calkins, 1994). The Writing Block begins with a 10-minute mini-lesson, during which the teacher writes and models all the things writers do. Next, the children do their own writing. They are at all different stages of the writing process—finishing a piece, starting a new piece, editing, illustrating, etc. While the children write, the teacher conferences with individuals who are getting ready to publish. This block ends with "Author's Chair" in which several students each day share work in progress or their published work.

The goals of the Writing Block are:

- To have students view writing as a way of telling about things.
- To develop fluent writing for all children.
- To teach students to use grammar and mechanics in their own writing.
- To teach particular writing forms.
- To allow students to learn to read through writing.
- To maintain the motivation and self-confidence of struggling writers.

Writing is the most multilevel block because it is not limited by the availability or acceptability of appropriate books. Because children are allowed to choose their own topics, whatever level of first-draft writing each child can accomplish is accepted, and students are allowed to work on their pieces as many days as needed, all children can succeed in writing. As teachers help children publish the piece they have chosen, they have the opportunity to truly "individualize" their teaching. Looking at the writing of the child usually reveals both what the child needs to move forward and what the child is ready to understand. The writing conference provides the "teachable moment," in which both advanced and struggling writers can be nudged forward in their literacy development.

Working with Words
In the Working with Words Block, children learn to read and spell high-frequency words and learn the patterns which allow them to decode and spell lots of words. The first 10-15 minutes of this block are usually given to reviewing the Word Wall words. Students practice new and old words daily by looking at them, saying them, chanting the letters, writing the words, and self-correcting the words with the teacher.

The remaining 15-25 minutes of words time is given to an activity which helps children learn to decode and spell. A variety of different activities are used on different days. Some of the most popular activities are Rounding Up the Rhymes, Making Words, Reading/Writing Rhymes, Using Words You Know, Word Sorting and Hunting, and Guess the Covered Word. (For grade-level specific descriptions of Working with Words activities, see *Month-by-Month Phonics for First Grade* by Cunningham & Hall, 1997; *Month-by-Month Phonics for Second Grade* by Hall & Cunningham, 1998; *Month-by-Month Phonics for Third Grade* by Cunningham & Hall, 1998; and *Month-by-Month Phonics for Upper Grades* by Cunningham & Hall, 1998.)

The goals of the Working with Words Block are:

- To teach children to read and spell high-frequency words.
- To teach children how to decode and spell lots of other words using patterns from known words.
- To have students automatically and fluently use phonics and spelling patterns while reading and writing.

Activities in the Working with Words Block are multilevel in a variety of ways. During the daily Word Wall practice, the children who have learned to read the words being practiced are learning to spell them. Other children who require lots of practice with words are learning to read the words.

Making Words, Rounding Up the Rhymes, Reading/Writing Rhymes, Using Words You Know, and other Working with Words Block activities are also multilevel. Most lessons begin with short, easy words and progress to longer, more complex words. Children who still need to develop phonemic awareness can do this as they decide which words rhyme and stretch out words. Each lesson includes some sorting of words into patterns, and then using those patterns to read and spell some new words. Children whose word knowledge is at all different levels see how they can use the patterns they see in words to read and spell other words. They also learn that rhyming words usually—but not always—have the same spelling pattern. All lessons provide review for beginning letter sounds for those who still need it.

Self-Selected Reading

Historically called "individualized reading" or "personalized reading" (Veatch, 1959), Self-Selected Reading is the time in the day when children read materials of their own choosing. The Self-Selected Reading Block includes (and usually begins with) a teacher read-aloud. Next, children read whatever they choose to read. While the children read, the teacher conferences with individual children about their reading. Opportunities are provided for children to share and respond to what is read.

This block is called Self-Selected Reading in order to emphasize the crucial importance of readers selecting what they want to read. Unfortunately, the initials for Self-Selected Reading (SSR) are the same as the initials for another common reading practice—Sustained Silent Reading. In Sustained Silent Reading, the teacher's role while the children read is to read something she enjoys reading. While having students see that the teacher enjoys reading is a worthwhile goal, we feel that having the teacher use this time to conference with individual children is a more productive use of the teacher's time.

The goals of the Self-Selected Reading Block are:
- To introduce children to all types of literature through the teacher read-aloud.
- To encourage children's reading interests.
- To provide instructional-level reading.
- To build intrinsic motivation for reading.

Self-Selected Reading is, by definition, multilevel. The component of Self-Selected Reading that makes it multilevel is the fact that children choose what they want to read. In Four-Blocks classrooms, teachers read aloud from all different types and levels of materials on all different topics, and then make the whole range of reading material available. During the weekly conferences, teachers support children's choices and help children choose books for the next week that they can read and will enjoy.

Self-Selected Reading in Building Blocks™ Classrooms

Because 30-40 minutes each day for each block is a basic principle, Four-Blocks is not an appropriate organizational framework for kindergarten. The kindergarten program is called Building Blocks™, and it integrates Guided Reading (shared reading of big books and charts), Self-Selected Reading, Writing, and Working with Words with the themes and units that are part of every kindergarten day. In kindergarten, the blocks don't have a set time slot—and certainly don't each get 30-40 minutes every day. Four-Blocks is a primary grades framework that is consistent with how primary teachers teach and schedule their day. Building Blocks is a kindergarten framework which is consistent with how kindergarten teachers teach and how they structure their day.

(For more about Building Blocks, see *Month-by-Month Reading and Writing for Kindergarten* by Hall & Cunningham, 1998; *The Teacher's Guide to Building Blocks™* by Hall & Williams, 2000; and the video, *Building Blocks™: A Framework for Reading and Writing in Kindergartens That Work* by Cunningham & Hall, 1996.)

Although Self-Selected Reading would not be scheduled for a 30-40 minute block of time each day in kindergarten, the components of the Self-Selected Reading Block are included in the kindergarten day. The teacher read-aloud is an important part of every kindergarten day and may happen at two or three different times in the day. Just as in Four-Blocks classrooms, Building Blocks teachers include a wide range of literature in their teacher read-aloud so that children will learn about all different kinds of books and begin to find their own reading interests. Even before most children can read any words, a short time is set aside each day for the children to "read books" on their own. Early in the year, this quiet reading time would probably only last for five minutes. By the end of the year, most Building Blocks classrooms would have 10 minutes each day for children to "read" books of their own choosing. Of course, many of the children are not really reading the books, at least not in the way older children and adults read books. They are reading books in the way young children read books—they pretend they can read! They talk to themselves (or a stuffed animal or younger child) about the pictures, and they make up wonderful stories! While these five-year-olds are "reading," the teacher goes around and holds quick conferences with them, sharing their delight in the book, and reading and talking about a few pages with each child.

Spending time with favorite books before they can actually read them is an activity engaged in at home by young children who then come to school and learn to "really read." In Building Blocks classrooms, teachers provide time each day for their kindergartners to read books in whatever way they can, and the teachers enjoy these books with them. In Chapter Six, you will see a description of the three ways young children read and how to encourage these emergent literacy behaviors in your kindergarten classroom.

Self-Selected Reading in Big Blocks™ Classrooms

Time allocation is also where the Four-Blocks® framework changes for upper grades. Because each block is viewed as an approach to reading, and because there are children in every Four-Blocks classroom for whom each block is their best road to literacy, beginning readers are taken down all four roads every day. However, by the time children have achieved a fluent third-grade reading and writing level, they read and write well enough that the time allocations can be changed.

Once children can read and write fluently at a third-grade level, they have well-developed phonics and spelling skills, so Working with Words no longer gets one-quarter of your literacy instructional time. The Working with Words instruction now focuses on big words, most of which come from science, health, and social studies. Guided Reading and Writing get longer blocks of time and may not necessarily happen every day. Much of Guided Reading and the focused-writing component of the Writing Block are integrated with the content subjects of science, health, and social studies. This integration provides more time for literacy and for these subject areas. Because this upper-grades framework focuses on big ideas and big words from subject areas, and includes big blocks of time for content integration, it is called Big Blocks™. (The best example of the Big Blocks™ framework can be found in the fourth-grade chapter of *Teachers in Action* by Cunningham, Moore, Cunningham & Moore, 2000 and in Chapter 10 of *Classrooms That Work* by Cunningham & Allington, 2002.)

Unfortunately, there are upper-grades classrooms in which most children do not read and write fluently at the third-grade level. Perhaps they have not gotten appropriate instruction, or have moved from school to school, or are just beginning to learn English. For these classrooms, the Four-Blocks, with its roughly equal instructional time allocated to each of the approaches, would still be the most appropriate and effective organizational framework. The issue is not the grade level of the students, but their reading levels. Until children read and write fluently at a third-grade level, they need a minimum of two hours of literacy instruction each day and equal attention to each of the four major approaches.

Regardless of whether your upper-grade students are mostly reading and writing at or above third-grade level, or mostly reading and writing at first- and second-grade levels, you will want to schedule a consistent 30-40 minutes block of time each day for Self-Selected Reading. Begin this block with a teacher read-aloud and then allow time for children to read books of their own choosing. While the children read, conference with individual children, trying to get to every child once a week. Schedule time for children to share books with one another—probably on a weekly or every-other-week basis.

The activities in the Self-Selected Reading Block are important for all children, but they may be most important for nine- to thirteen-year-olds. These preteen years are a "critical period" in which children either become readers or they don't.

In a recent research study, Ivey and Broaddus (2001) surveyed 1,765 sixth graders to determine what motivates them to read. The responses of this large group of diverse preteens indicated that their major motivation for reading came from having time for independent reading in books of their own choosing and teachers reading aloud to them.

All children in this age range have some reading ability, but unfortunately, many children—including some very able readers—do not have the reading habit. There comes a point in the development of any skill where you know the basics and just need a "lot of practice" to become good and automatic at it. The best readers are the ones who read the most. Children who have discovered "their books and authors" read more—in and out of school—than children who just read what they are assigned to read.

It is ironic that at the very age when children can most profit from being inspired by the teacher read-aloud and the book sharing of their peers, these activities often get omitted because "there is no time." In upper-grade classrooms with a wide variety of books, there is something everyone can enjoy and learn from. Avid readers can digest books at their advanced levels. Struggling readers can read books and magazines that interest them. The intermediate and middle grades are a critical time in the development of the reading habit for avid and struggling readers alike. If we are serious about teaching every child to read as well as they possibly can, we must find the time for Self-Selected Reading each and every day in our intermediate and middle grades classrooms.

Connecting Self-Selected Reading to the Other Blocks and the Rest of the Curriculum

Each block has its scheduled time in every classroom, but Four-Blocks teachers also make many links among the four different blocks and to other areas of the curriculum. Some of the links most commonly made for the Self-Selected Reading Block include:

- Reading aloud to children, during the first part of Self-Selected Reading, a selection which "sets them up" for an author, genre or topic they will soon be reading during Guided Reading.
- Making books read during Guided Reading book club groups available for children to choose during Self-Selected Reading.
- Choosing a topic for the writing minilesson which relates to something read during the teacher read-aloud portion of Self-Selected Reading.
- Choosing materials for the teacher read-aloud that fit the theme or relate to a science, health, or social studies topic.
- Making available during Self-Selected Reading a variety of materials on different levels which fit science, health, and social studies topics.

You are probably thinking right now that the reading materials are a crucial part of the Self-Selected Reading Block and wondering about what to use, how to choose materials, and where to get them. In the next chapter, you will learn about materials and how to use everything you have, not to mention what you can beg, borrow, and contrive!

3

MATERIALS FOR SELF-SELECTED READING

Four Blocks® eliminates the need for reams of duplicator paper and running off worksheets, but poses a new problem, namely, "How do I get more books for my classroom? My children are reading everything they can get their hands on!" What a wonderful problem for teachers and schools to have! In this chapter, you will see the many ways that individual teachers and schools have solved this dilemma and where you can find the books and materials you need and want in your classrooms for the Self-Selected Reading Block.

Teachers who enjoy this block usually have lots of books in their own personal library that they delight in reading to their students, and also have lots of books for their students to read. In fact, meeting all the goals of the Self-Selected Reading Block is impossible if you do not have a variety of books to read to your children and a good collection of children's books and materials from which the children can choose to read. Of course, all the books need to be organized in some way. Teachers use plastic crates, dishpans, baskets, racks, and shelves to do this so that their students can easily see the books available and have easy access to them. Fortunately, most schools have libraries or media centers from which teachers can borrow books and extend their own personal collections. There is also the local public library from which books can be borrowed free of charge—all you need is a library card, which is also free. When you want more children's books than you own, you can start with these two sources.

Teachers add to their personal collections with books purchased from school and PTA funds, although these books usually belong to the school, grade level, or classroom, not the teacher. Garage sales and children's book clubs are two inexpensive sources of additional books for elementary teachers.

As mentioned in the last chapter, the goals for the Self-Selected Reading Block are:

- To introduce children to all types of literature through the teacher read-aloud.
- To encourage children's reading interests.
- To provide instructional-level reading.
- To build intrinsic motivation for reading.

All Types of Literature—Fiction and Nonfiction

It is obvious that if you are going to introduce children to all types of literature, then you must read aloud to children from all different types of books. Let's begin by reminding ourselves of all the different genres of literature for children. (You may want to search your brain or your basement for your old "kiddie lit" files!)

Fiction is made up; it didn't happen! For some kinds of fiction—realistic fiction, historical fiction, and mysteries—it could have happened, but it didn't. Other types of fiction, including folk and fairy tales, science fiction, and fantasy, are made up and probably couldn't happen. Animals don't talk; fairy godmothers don't turn pumpkins into coaches; and there is no technology (as of now) for beaming people to faraway places. Fiction is almost always some kind of story and has the elements of a story. There is a setting and some characters. The characters interact and do something. They have goals or solve problems. There is action and plot and drama! We need to read stories, so that our students can follow the story structure and think about the characters, settings, events, and conclusions. Children need to think about why things happen and why characters behave in the ways that they do.

Nonfiction could and did happen. Nonfiction includes informational books about animals, sports, places, art, cooking, gardening, health, and a host of other topics we can learn about through reading. Nonfiction also includes biographies and autobiographies. Informational reading requires different comprehension skills and strategies from story reading—and different listening skills. In order to remember and learn from informational selections, you often have to figure out and remember the sequence in which important events occurred. Events that follow one another often cause each other and you need to think about what causes what to happen. Often, several things—animals, people, events, places, etc.—are compared and contrasted, and you have to summarize and draw conclusions about the similarities and differences. Informational text contains special features, such as headings, bold print, maps, charts, and glossaries. These special features are there to help comprehension, but they only help during a read-aloud if the teacher shows and explains them. (Example: "Here is a plant with its parts labeled....") Children also have to learn to look at these features when reading alone.

Even within fiction and nonfiction, there are differences in the types of books you can choose. The best books for children win the approval of critics and children, as well as teachers. Children today are more sophisticated and knowledgeable than any other generation. The books you read to them should appeal to and represent the many and varied children in your classrooms today—their backgrounds, their interests, and their past and present experiences. Here is a look at some of the many different kinds of children's literature available for teachers and children to read:

Picture Books
Pictures books can be appealing at every grade level, and they give students a chance to enjoy both the story and illustrations. Picture books are often written by the same person who illustrates the book, but not always. We have all had a terrible, horrible, no good, very bad day like Alexander in *Alexander and the Terrible, Horrible, No Good, Very Bad Day* by Judith Viorst, and that picture

thinking about their own relatives when the teacher reads books like *The Relatives Came* by Cynthia Rylant.

Wordless Books

Some picture books are wordless and invite the readers to tell their own stories using the pictures. When teachers use wordless books and tell stories, they model this process for their young students. Some examples of wordless books are Mercer Mayer's books about Frog. Anyone and everyone can read a wordless book! For older children, they are excellent to use as springboards for story writing.

Mother Goose and Nursery Rhymes

These are often called "lap books" because a young child's first experience with books is usually associated with being held in the lap of a loving adult. For many children, Mother Goose was their first introduction to the world of children's literature. Much of the appeal of Mother Goose and nursery rhymes lies in the musical quality of the varied language patterns and the rhythm and rhyme of the verses. They also tell a story in a few lines and have interesting, unusual, likeable characters like Little Miss Muffet, Humpty Dumpty, and Old King Cole. Teachers can choose among many beautifully illustrated Mother Goose editions. There is no one "best" Mother Goose book; it is a matter of personal preference.

ABC Books

Alphabet books are fun to read to young children and are best when they present only one or two objects on a page. These objects should be easily identifiable and meaningful for the children to whom you are reading. Most books contain vivid, full-color photographs or illustrations. *Paddington's ABC* by Michael Bond and *By the Sea: An Alphabet Book* by Ann Blades are examples of two easy ABC books with just a picture and one word for each letter of the alphabet. Some alphabet books are written in rhyme and help our youngest students develop phonemic awareness. *Animalia* by Graeme Base and *An Alphabet Book of Cats and Dogs* by Sheila Moxley are two ABC books that are written as tongue twisters and are fun to read—and even more fun if you are the listener! Do not overlook ABC books for older readers, like *NBA Action from A to Z* by James Preller and *Basketball ABC: The NBA Alphabet* by Florence Cassen Mayers . After listening to an alphabet book, children can make their own ABC books, such as an "ABC of Animals" or an "ABC of Pioneer Life."

Concept and Counting Books

Concept books teach something—colors, shapes, numbers, opposites, etc. These books are popular for preschool and kindergarten children. Counting books provide young children with pictures for counting instead of objects. Ideally, boys and girls should learn to count by playing with real objects such as blocks, boxes, buttons, or model cars.

Folk Tales and Fairy Tales

Folk tales and fairy tales have been handed down through the years, first in oral and then in written form. *The Three Pigs*, *The Three Bears*, *The Three Billy Goats Gruff*, and the *The Gingerbread Boy* are examples of folk tales often read to young children. *Snow White* and *Cinderella* are examples of fairy tales, usually read to children who are a little older. In these stories, time and place is established quickly, with "Once upon a time . . ." or a similar line. The purpose of these tales is usually to tell an entertaining story. Often dialect enhances these stories; and power, hard work, and love and/or kindness are often the themes.

Fantasy

Fantasy is not real and usually means more than it says. Underlying most fantasy is a comment on the society at the time the book was written. Children vary in their capacity to understand and find the hidden meanings in a story. A child's taste for fantasy may be developed when a teacher reads aloud a book like A. A. Milne's *Winnie-the-Pooh*. Books of modern fantasy are usually longer than fairy tales and contain some imaginary elements that are contrary to reality as we know it. For example, they may contain personification of animals, such as in *Charlotte's Web* by E. B. White, or toys as in *Winnie-the-Pooh*. They may create new worlds, such as Narnia in *The Lion, the Witch, and the Wardrobe* by C.S. Lewis, or change the size of human beings as in *Indian in the Cupboard* by Lynne Reid Banks. Or, they may give humans unusual powers as in *The Chocolate Touch* by Patrick Skene Catling, or manipulate time patterns as in *A Wrinkle in Time* by Madeline L'Engle. Teachers need to read fantasy so students can listen and imagine a different world and infer the rules the characters in that world live by. The popularity of J. K. Rowling's *Harry Potter* books illustrates the popularity of fantasy with readers of all ages.

Realistic Fiction, Historical Fiction, and Contemporary Fiction

Realistic fiction may be defined as that imaginative writing which accurately reflects life as it was lived in the past or could be lived today. Everything in the story could have happened to real people in this world. Historical fiction portrays life as it may have been lived in the past. Contemporary fiction focuses upon the problems of life today. Children of divorce, alienated and abused children, developing friendships, finding one's self, stories of survival, physical disabilities, racism, and death and dying are just some of the subjects about which many contemporary fiction books are written today.

Sports—Fiction and Nonfiction

Children today are energetic participants and spectators in a variety of individual and team sports. Sports are "in," and books on sports are in demand. Fiction, biographies, and informational books about sports extend and enrich children's personal experiences. It is difficult to find many well-written sports stories, but children select these books because they are personally involved and interested in these activities. It is easier to find biographies of sports stars and informational books on how to play the different games.

Poetry

Poetry communicates experience by appealing to both the thoughts and feelings of its reader or listener. How are children ever going to enjoy poetry if teachers do not expose them to the different poets and styles by reading poetry to them? Young children respond to both the rhyme and rhythm of a poem. Rhyme is one aspect of sound; alliteration, or the repetition of an initial sound, is another. Children also need to be freed from the notion that all poetry must rhyme in order to be poetry. They should be introduced to some poetry that doesn't rhyme, such as free verse and haiku. Every teacher will want to own at least one excellent anthology of poetry for children, as well as several books of children's favorite poems by such authors as Lee Bennett Hopkins or Shel Silverstein.

Informational Books

Certainly there are more informational books for children, on a wider variety of topics, than ever before. At one time, when children (and teachers) wanted information, they went to the encyclopedia. Today's informational books are more inviting, more attractive, and better suited to leisure reading than study. Book jackets and book reviews often tell us the age range, reading level, or interest level of the content. Children will often read "beyond their abilities" when reading a book about a subject they are interested in and want to learn more about. Children will also turn to difficult books if they have lots of pictures or diagrams. At the same time, vocabulary, sentence length, size of type, and the organization of the book are factors to be considered. When children see crowded pages, relatively small type, and few pictures, they may reject a book with useful information. Informational books should be interesting to the eye as well as being informational. You will want to find as many informational books as possible about any themes and topics your class is studying.

Biography

Children read biographies as they read fiction—for the story or plot. Children usually want a biography to be written as a story, not a collection of facts, events, and dates. Children like to look to the past and find out about the people who lived great lives, like Abraham Lincoln, Martin Luther King, Jr., Benjamin Franklin, Helen Keller, and Harriet Tubman. Many children like reading the biographies of "real" (live) people even better than dead ones! Today, it is easy to find biographies of sports heroes (Michael Jordan, Kobe Bryant, Tiger Woods, Mark McGwire, and Mia Hamm), presidents and politicians (Bill Clinton and George W. Bush), and performers (Bill Cosby, Whitney Houston, and Tom Hanks). There are also picture-book biographies (David Adler has written many wonderful ones!), including simplified biographies for beginning readers with limited vocabulary, and biographies for more sophisticated, elementary school-aged readers.

Easy Chapter Books

Easy chapter books are wonderful for first- and second-graders who have learned to read and want to read chapter books just like their older siblings. They are also perfect for reluctant readers who want to have a chapter book in their hand but are not ready for a novel of any length. These easy chapter books, many of them belonging to series, have become loved by students at all grade levels in the past few years. *Junie B. Jones* books, the *Magic Tree House* series, and the *Captain Underpants* books come to mind quickly when teachers talk about the new, easy chapter books that children like to listen to and read themselves during Self-Selected Reading.

Mysteries

Children, like adults, love a good mystery. We need to read mysteries so that children can learn to watch for clues and draw conclusions. Mysteries have won more state children's choice awards than any other type of story (Lynch-Brown & Tomlinson, 1999). The element of suspense is a strong part of the appeal of these stories. There are mysteries for beginning readers, like *Encyclopedia Brown* by Donald J. Sobol, and mysteries for the more advanced readers in the upper grades, like *Doll House Murders* by Betty Ren Wright.

Multicultural Books

Today's children are growing up in a multicultural society in which understanding and appreciating differences is important. It is essential that we learn to respect and appreciate the diversity of all cultures within our society. Books can never substitute for firsthand experiences, but they can raise the consciousness level of children and deepen their understanding of cultures that are different from their own. Multicultural books are those in which the main characters are from racial, language, religious, or ethnic minorities, such as African-Americans, Asian-Americans, Hispanics, Jewish-Americans, or Native Americans. (*Yellow Bird and Me* and *The Gift Giver* by Joyce Hansen are two examples of books about cultural diversity.) Each year, more and more authors and illustrators of multicultural books are recognized for their contributions to children's literature.

Award Winners

The Caldecott Medal is given each year to the illustrator of a children's picture book. (See pages 117-128 for a list of previous winners.) The Newbery Medal is given each year to the author of the most distinguished contribution to children's literature. (See pages 129-144 for a list of previous winners.) There are also awards for juvenile mystery (Edgar Allen Poe Award), historical fiction (Scott O'Dell Award), nonfiction (Orbis Pictus Award), and for African-American authors and illustrators who promote peace and harmony in children's books (Coretta Scott King Award). Teachers need to include some of these award-winning books—and the runners-up—in their reading materials; these books represent some of the best in children's literature each year.

Magazines

There are hundreds of magazines available for children. Magazines about drama, geography, health, history, language (in different languages), language arts, literature, math, recreation, and science are available for children, with a paid subscription. Some of the most popular are: *Humpty Dumpty's Magazine, Jack and Jill, Children's Digest, Cricket, Scholastic Math, Ranger Rick,* and *3-2-1 Contact.*

Weekly Magazines

Magazines such as *Weekly Reader* and *Scholastic News* can be a wonderful source of reading material to include in your Self-Selected Reading Block. When classrooms get a set each week, a few copies can be put in the book baskets or magazine rack. The selections included in these weekly magazines are usually informational, along with an occasional play or poem. They also often include directions for making something or doing some kind of experiment. The reading, accompanied by lots of visuals, is highly motivating for many of your readers who like to read and get information, including struggling readers.

Weekly Reader (200 First Stamford Place, P.O. Box 120023, Stamford, CT 06912, *www.weeklyreader.com*, 1-800- 446-3355) and *Scholastic News* (P.O. Box 7503, Jefferson City, MO 65102-9966, *www.scholastic.com*, 1-800-631-1586) cost about $4.00 per child per year if you order at least 10 copies. You also get a desk copy free! *Time for Kids* (Time, Inc., 1271 Avenue of the Americas, New York, NY 10020, *www.timeforkids.com*, 1-800-777-8600) now also publishes a student weekly magazine.

Gender and Preference

According to a national survey, bookstores sell 80% of their fiction titles to women and 80% of their nonfiction titles to men! Considering that some women buy an occasional informational book along with "novels," and some men buy and read stories, and women buy books as gifts for the men in their lives and vice versa, this is an astonishing statistic! There seems to be a clear preference for females toward fiction and for males toward nonfiction in the adult American reading population. Now, consider the type of reading material that elementary teachers—who are overwhelmingly female—provide for their students and the generally less-positive attitudes of boys toward reading and ask yourselves if there might be a connection here. Could it be that most of what we read to and make available to our students to read is fiction or a story of some sort, and what many boys would rather be listening to and reading is information?

Regardless of gender, people have different preferences about what they read. Adult readers tend to favor one or two types of books and do most of their reading within those categories. When choosing books to read aloud to children, try to read from "all the different sections of the bookstore." That way you know that every child will have the opportunity to hear and discover the type of book that grabs him (or her!).

When we looked at what teachers and students were using for the Guided Reading Block, we found a huge amount of realistic fiction, folk/fairy tales and fantasy, some poetry and informational science books (mostly about animals), and very little or none of the other types. We then began "begging, borrowing, and contriving" so that our Guided Reading Block provided a more balanced reading diet. Teachers can do the same in Self-Selected Reading by surveying the books in their personal and classroom libraries and finding ways to beg, borrow, and somehow obtain books on a variety of levels in all the different genres.

Where Do I Get These Books?

To achieve all the goals of the Self-Selected Reading Block, you must collect and use the widest range of materials possible. You may be thinking, "Easy for you to say! I don't have many books because I'm a new teacher," "I just changed to a new grade level, and I have almost no chapter (or easy, picture, etc.) books," or, " I just started teaching and my budget is limited. I like children's books, but I do not have many." Here are some ways for clever teachers to add to their collections:

Library
Talk to the librarian at the local public library or at your school library or media center. Their business is to know which books children like and which books children are reading. Their advice is priceless, and they have books right there to hand you. Send notes to your librarian, saying something like, "We have looked for books about spiders and can't find any in our classroom. Do you have any in the library or know where we could find out more about them?"

School Book Clubs

Some publishers sell books through classrooms. Children receive an order form with descriptions of the books available, and they choose the books they want to purchase. The teacher passes out these order blanks, collects them after they go home, tallies the order, and sends it to the company. The books are usually available at a discount price. Each book order comes with "special" books at "special" prices. These specials are often just what the teacher and students really want. Teachers can often get free books based on the quantity of books their students purchase. If a teacher purchases a certain monetary amount with the first book offer, she gets "bonus points" that can be used for even more books. Clever teachers have explained to us how they purchase books for themselves and get hundreds of extra books each year for their personal and classroom libraries this way.

Home and Mail Order Book Clubs

Several direct mail booksellers send descriptions of books to your home. You can join book clubs that are geared to the ages of your children at home or the children you teach. One kindergarten teacher got all her Dr. Seuss books at a good price by joining a child's book club. Since she was young, single, and childless, she signed up an "imaginary" child, giving him a name she would want to use one day for a "real" child.

Book Stores and Toy Stores

Bookstores make a business of knowing which books kids like. Knowledgeable clerks in reputable stores know that if they sell you a really good book, you and your fellow teachers, and probably some friends and neighbors, will be back for more. They carry the latest and greatest books and can use their computer to find out what is available and how fast they can get a book in if it's not in stock. Ask for discounts! Bookstores often offer teachers 10-20% off the listed price, so carry your school identification badge (many schools now have these), a paycheck stub, an insurance card, or some means to identify yourself as a teacher so you can get an "Educator's Discount Card." Then, use this discount every time you buy hardback or paperback books for classroom purposes.

Many grocery stores, discount stores, novelty stores, drug stores, museums, and children's toy stores also carry books. You may need to look carefully at the offerings, but there is no shortage of places to buy children's books.

School Book Fairs

Some Parent Teacher Associations (PTA) or Organizations (PTO) hold book fairs at school to raise money for school needs, and this includes books! This is a good place to pick up books. Spend plenty of time exploring the display racks and make a list before you buy. Often the PTA will let you purchase books at discount prices or get a predetermined amount for your classroom. Some schools have teachers make wish lists of books, and parents can buy from these lists for their children's teacher(s). Sometimes book fairs offer secondhand books at unbelievable prices. These books are "used," but your students will still enjoy "using" them even more!

On-Line Stores

Books can be bought from on-line bookstores, like Amazon.com, which offer delivery in a day or two. Some on-line bookstores also offer "specials" on favorite books and/or authors; look for these! With on-line stores, you can easily see what books are available and in stock. Just like going to the library and searching for a book, on these sites you go on a virtual search of books by title, subject, or author. As you shop on the Web, you can "add the books to your shopping cart" and pay with your credit card at "checkout" time. Many people prefer this method of book shopping because it saves time.

Family, Neighbors, and Friends

One way to significantly increase the number of books in the classroom library is to collect used books from family, neighbors, and friends. Many families have a stack of books that their children have long outgrown which they would be glad to donate to your classroom. One clever teacher needed books for her classroom, so she put an announcement in her church bulletin. In the announcement, she said she needed used books for her first-grade classroom and that a box would be in the church lobby the following Sunday for anyone who wanted to donate books. This teacher came away from church that next Sunday with over 200 children's books for her classroom! She then invited several parents to an after-school "book browsing party," where the parents went through the books to make sure they were appropriate for first-graders and in good enough condition to be placed in the classroom.

Skinny Books from Old Basals

In many school systems, after new basals are adopted, the old basal texts can be cut apart and "skinny" books made with the selections you deem "worthful." (This is a wonderful project for a parent volunteer who wants to be helpful, but can't help with a big project, or for someone who wants to help, but is homebound.) Selections which are easy, delightful, and able to link to some other part of your curriculum score a perfect "10" and get included as "skinny" Self-Selected Reading books!

Organizing and Storing Books

First, let us say there is no one right way to organize your books for Self-Selected Reading. What works for you is probably the best way for you. But, if you do not have a clue as to what to do with all your books, here are some ideas. Books can be stored on shelves, in rubber or plastic bins or crates, or in dishpans on a shelf.

Some teachers organize their books by authors (Eric Carle books, Leo Leonni books, etc.) or favorite characters (Arthur books, Clifford books, Encyclopedia Brown books, etc.), by themes (animal books, books about friends, hilarious stories, etc.), or by all of these categories.

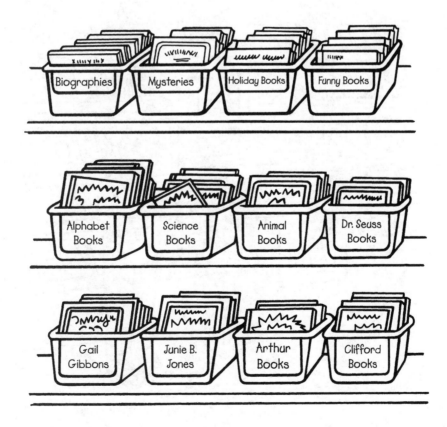

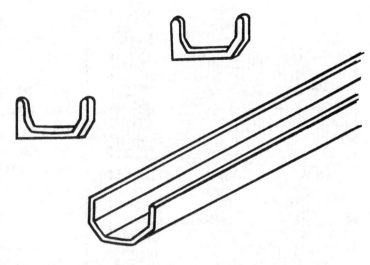

We know that children most often select books that are displayed face-out on shelves or on a display table or shelf. Children are probably attracted to these books because they think that the teacher believes that these are "special" books. Finding unique, efficient ways to display books in the classroom is a challenge. Here is a wonderful way to display lots of books while using very little classroom space. The key is "rain gutter" that is sold in home improvement or hardware stores. Rain gutters are made of plastic, are very inexpensive, and come in a range of colors. As you can see in the illustrations, the gutters can be arranged along a wall using support brackets to hold dozens of books. The gutters protect the books and let you bless a lot of books by placing them face-out in these special "book holders."

Do I Need to Level Books?

Leveling books in a Four-Blocks classroom is not necessary unless you want to, can, and have the time to do it. Some first-grade teachers find this helps them know if children are reading books at the right level. One teacher told us an easy way to level all the books in your classroom. First, divide all the books you have into three groups by how hard or easy each book will be for most of the children in your class. Then, rate each book as "easy," "hard," or "just right," and label the books accordingly with colorful adhesive dots (green = easy, red = just right, and yellow = hard).

Some teachers level their books for Self-Selected Reading using any of the many published books or Web sites that help teachers do this. *Guiding Readers and Writers Grades 3-6* (Fountas and Pinnell, 2001), *Matching Books To Readers* (Fountas and Pinnell, 1999), and *Guided Reading* (Fountas and Pinnell, 1996) are three books that do this. All have descriptions of the different levels, but *Guided Reading* also has illustrations of most levels that you might find helpful. Also, there are several on-line sites that level books:

http://204.98.1.2/isu/langarts/bklst.html

http://teachers.pps.k12.or.us:591/leveled_books/search.htm

http://www.1ststepsintoreading.com/database.htm

http://www.leveledbooks.com

http://expage.com/page/kikiteachersleveledbooklinks

Some teachers are not that organized and recoil at the thought of having to level all the thousands of books they have in their classrooms, especially if they have to look up the level of each book. However, most teachers do try to match books to the students in their class by interest and ability. They keep books together by topic and sometimes by levels, but not in a strict sense (like emergent readers from Wright Group, easy chapter books, challenging books, etc.). The goal for Four-Blocks teachers is to help students find books they CAN read and WILL enjoy. If there are students during Self-Selected Reading who don't have books they can read, teachers simply grab a few emergent readers (or the crate) and let the students choose one or two books that interest them. Four-Blocks teachers often tell us that they make sure to read aloud several of these easy readers each week and talk about the illustrations and the humor in the story. They "bless" books written on the lowest levels and help the students feel safe choosing these books to read. Because Four-Blocks teachers conference with their students every week, they know if the students are reading books that are "just right." They also know what books their students enjoy and why they choose the books they do.

Publishers

Who is publishing what? At one time schools bought very little besides basal readers for children. With the advent of "literature-based curriculum," many basal companies went out of business, and many companies, big and small, started selling children's books to schools. There is no way this list could possibly encompass all the companies out there. There are many publishing companies that sell their own books, and many other companies that sell books from several publishers. Also, many publishers have bought or merged with other publishers, and it is hard to keep up with this trend (Sort of like banks!).

Here is a list of some of the companies that offer children's books to schools and parents:

Abdo Publishing Company
Address: 4940 Viking Drive, Suite 622, Edina, MN 55435
Phone: 1-800-800-1312
Web site: *www.abdopub.com*
What's Available: Alphabet books; phonics books; concept books; animal books; books about different periods of history; biographies of presidents, inventors, authors, sports stars, and heroes; mysteries; and some of the "classics."

Crabtree Publishing Company
Address: PMB 16A, 350 Fifth Ave., Suite 3308, NY, NY 10118
Phone: 1-800-387-7650
Web site: *www.crabtreebooks.com*
What's Available: Books on world cultures, multicultural studies, space, nature, animals, sports, biographies, arts and crafts, farming, and books for beginning readers.

Holiday House Publishing Company
Address: 425 Madison Avenue, New York, NY 10017
Phone: 1-212-688-0085
Web site: *www.holidayhouse.com*
What's Available: Award-winning books from popular authors, such as David Adler, Gail Gibbons, Tomie DePaola, Myra Livingston Cohn, Steven Kroll, Virginia Driving Hawke Sneve, Betty Ren Wright, and others.

Little, Brown and Company
Address: 3 Center Plaza, Boston, MA 02108-2084
Phone: 1-800-759-0190
Web site: *www.twbookmark.com/childrens*
What's Available: Picture books, board books, novelty books, *Arthur* books, many of the award-winning and honor books, sports books, holiday books, biographies, and more.

National Geographic Society
Address: P. O. Box 98199, Washington, DC 20090-8199
Phone: 1-800-647-5463
Web site: www.nationalgeographic.com
What's Available: Lots of informational books including informational big books.

Newbridge
Address: P. O. Box 1270, Littleton, MA 01460
Phone: 1-800-867-0307
Web site: *www.newbridgeonline.com*
What's Available: Nonfiction for Guided Reading; social studies, science, and mathematics for emergent readers, early readers, and students in the intermediate grades. Their catalog also contains big books, student books, and teachers guides organized by themes under the headings Science, Math, and Social Studies.

Oxford University Press
Address: 2001 Evans Road, Cary, NC 27513-2009
Phone: 1-800-451-7556
Web site: www.oup-usa.org
What's Available: Wordless books; Red/Green/Blue Oxford Readers; multicultural stories; take-home books; books of rhymes; and books written in Spanish.

Rand McNally
Address: P. O. Box 678-7263, Skokie, IL 60076-9714
Phone: 1-800-678-7263
Web site: *www.k12online.com*
What's Available: Nonfiction in social studies, science, history, and geography.

Random House Books for Young Readers
Address: 400 Hahn Road, Westminster, MD 21157
Phone: 1-800-726-0600
Web site: *www.randomhouse.com/kids* and *www.randomhouse.com/teachers*
What's available: Paperback and hardcover copies of popular books/series for young readers about characters like Arthur, the Berenstein Bears, Dragon Tales, Junie B. Jones, Magic Tree House, Sesame Street, Seussville, Star Wars, Sweet Valley, and more. Also award-winning picture books and children's novels published by Bantam, Doubleday, and Dell.

Rigby
Address: P.O. Box 797, Crystal Lake, IL 60039-0797
Phone: 1-800-822-8661
Web site: *www.rigby.com*
What's Available: Big books, Rigby PM Collection, Rigby PM Plus, fiction and nonfiction books with titles grouped by theme.

Scholastic Books
Address: P. O. Box 7502, 2931 East McCarty Street, Jefferson City, MO 65102
Phone: 1-800-Scholastic (1-800-724-6527)
Web site: *www.scholastic.com*
What's Available: A wealth of award-winning and honor book; hardcover and paperback picture books; children's novels (K-9); poetry books; fiction and nonfiction; reference books for children; *Magic School Bus* and *Clifford* books series. (Books are listed by authors and titles and are available to teachers at discount prices.)

Simon & Schuster Children's Publishing
Address: 1230 Avenue of the Americas, New York, NY 10020
Phone: 1-800-223-2336
Web site: *www.simonsayskids.com*
What's Available: Hardback and paperback books, including Aladdin Paperbacks, picture books, holiday books, books on sports, concept books, and board books.

Steck-Vaughn Co.
Address: 4515 Seton Center Parkway, Suite 300, Austin, TX 78759
Phone: 1-512-343-8227
Web site: *www.steck-vaughn.com*
What's Available: Supplementary reading materials for early literacy including the "pair-it" books pairing a fiction and nonfiction book about the same topic for children.

Sundance
Address: P.O. Box 1326, Littleton, MA 01460
Phone: 1-800-343-8204
Web site: *www.sundancepub.com*
What's available: Alphabet books; emergent readers; leveled readers; early chapter books; paired fiction and nonfiction books; nonfiction for emergent readers; nonfiction titles in social studies and science at a variety of levels; classroom libraries; and individual paperback titles.

Albert Whitman & Company
Address: 6240 Oakton Street, Morton Grove, IL 60053
Phone: 1-800-255-7675
Web site: www.albertwhitman.com
What's Available: A variety of children's books, including *The Boxcar Children's Mysteries*.

Wright Group/McGraw-Hill (Wright Group has been bought by McGraw-Hill.)
Address: 19201 120th Avenue, Bothell, WA 98011-9512
Phone: 1-800-648-2970
Web site: *www.wrightgroup.com*
What's Available: Big books; Sunshine Books; Storybox books; emergent readers on social studies and science topics; Joy Cowley books; traditional stories; and poems.

Authors' Sites

Many teachers want to know more about their favorite authors and what books they are publishing. Here are some Web sites that do just that:

www.tooter4kids.com/Classroom/favorite_author_sites.htm

www.cbcbooks.org/html/links.html

Tedd Arnold	www.geocities.com/Athens/Delphi/9096/
Jim Aylesworth	www.ayles.com
Judy Blume	www.judyblume.com
Jan Brett	www.janbrett.com
Norman Birdwell (Clifford)	www.scholastic.com/clifford/index.htm
Marc Brown (Arthur)	www.pbs.org/arthur *and*
	www.randomhouse.com/kids/arthur
Eric Carle	www.eric-carle.com
Joanna Cole	www.scholastic.com/magicschoolbus/home.htm
Beverly Cleary	www.beverlycleary.com
Tomie DePaola	www.tomie.com
Mem Fox	www.memfox.net
Gail Gibbons	www.gailgibbons.com/
Joan Holub	www.joanholub.com
Ann Martin	www.scholastic.com/annmartin/bsc/index.htm
Bill Martin Jr.	www.tiill.com/bill.htm
Bruce McMillan	www.brucemcmillan.com
Bernard Most	www.bernardmost.com
Mary Pope Osborne	www.randomhouse.com/kids/magictreehouse
Katherine Paterson	www.terabithia.com
Barbara Parks	www.randomhouse.com/kids/junieb
Dav Pilkey	www.pilkey.com
Daniel Pinkwater	www.pinkwater.com
Patricia Polacco	www.patriciapolacco.com
Robert Quackenbush	www.rquackenbush.com
J.K. Rowling	www.scholastic.com/harrypotter/index.htm
John Scieszka and Lane Smith	www.baloneyhenryp.com
Dr. Seuss	www.randomhouse.com/seussville
Janet Stevens	www.janetstevens.com

Rosemary Wells	www.rosemarywells.com
David Wisniewski	www.eduplace.com/rdg/author/wisniewski/index.html
Audrey Wood	www.audreywood.com
Jane Yolen	www.janeyolen.com
Chris Van Allsburg	www.eduplace.com/rdg/author/cva/index.html

The next chapter will help you understand the importance of reading aloud to children the books you have—or the books you are going to get. Teachers need to read aloud every day. No matter what the pressure is on you or your grade level, YOU and your children cannot afford not to do Self-Selected Reading every day, including the teacher read-aloud. Read on!

4

WHY SELF-SELECTED READING?

In Four-Blocks® classrooms, there are four major goals for the Self-Selected Reading Block:

- To introduce children to all types of literature
- To encourage children's reading interests
- To provide instructional-level reading
- To build intrinsic motivation for reading

Self-Selected Reading is multilevel because children choose what they want to read. In Four-Blocks classrooms, teachers read aloud and share a variety of reading materials at different reading levels during Self-Selected Reading. Teachers share reading materials on a wide range of topics to expose students to a variety of topics and genres. In Four-Blocks classrooms, Self-Selected Reading is viewed as an essential component of the instructional program with specific time allotted to Self-Selected Reading each and every day. Weekly conferences allow the teacher to assist and support students in their book choices, and can provide the teacher with important information about each child's reading development. While a rich classroom library is the foundation for a successful Self-Selected Reading Block, it is what Four-Blocks teachers do to support and sustain Self-Selected Reading that creates the payoff in terms of increasing reading proficiency and building intrinsic motivation to read.

How Self-Selected Reading Increases Reading Proficiency

There are so many things that teachers must do during the day. Teaching schedules are busier than ever before. Sometimes, Self-Selected Reading is the first thing to go when there is time pressure, either because there is the feeling that time must be spent teaching skills that will be assessed, or because the value of time spent reading and its relationship to increased reading proficiency is not well understood. This is unfortunate because there is strong evidence that a well-balanced reading program MUST include time for children to practice reading. Does time spent reading during Self-Selected Reading result in increased reading achievement? The research suggests that the answer to this important question is a resounding "YES!" Linehart, Zigmond, and Cooley (1981) found that time spent in silent reading was positively related to gains in reading achievement. Anderson, Wilson, and Fielding (1988) reported that ten minutes a day of sustained reading of trade books was associated with sharp gains in reading achievement. Research by Reutzel and Hollingsworth (1991) found that sustained reading of trade books was as effective as comprehension skills instruction in increasing reading comprehension. In summary, the research suggests that engaging students in the practice of reading is a primary means for improving reading comprehension.

The More You Read, the Better You Read

We know that in the early development of the reading process, struggling readers who have difficulty in decoding begin to have less exposure to text than do more proficient readers (Allington, 1984). These struggling readers often find themselves in instructional materials that are too difficult for them to read (Allington, 1984; Gambrell, Wilson, & Gantt, 1981). The combination of poor decoding skills, difficult instructional materials, and lack of adequate practice reading texts often results in frustrating early reading experiences for these students. According to Cunningham and Stanovich (1998), lack of exposure and practice delays the development of fluency and word recognition skills. Thus, reading comprehension is hindered, frustrating reading experiences increase, and practice is avoided. Stanovich (1986) has termed this the "Matthew Effect." This term is taken from the biblical passage that describes the rich-get-richer and poor-get-poorer phenomenon. In reading, good readers tend to have more practice reading and, consequently, get better and better at reading. Poor readers, on the other hand, spend less time reading and have fewer experiences with appropriate-level reading materials.

Reading Makes You Smarter

There is clear evidence from reading research that the amount of time spent reading (reading volume) is the major contributor to increased vocabulary development and reading proficiency (Allington, 1983; Hayes & Ahrens, 1988; Nagy & Anderson, 1984; Stanovich, 1986). According to Cunningham and Stanovich (1998), reading has cognitive benefits beyond getting meaning from the page. Their research indicates that children who get off to a good start in reading are more likely to read more as they progress through the grades. Furthermore, the very act of reading can help children compensate for modest levels of cognitive ability by increasing their vocabulary and general knowledge. An important finding from this research is that ability is not the only variable that counts in the development of intelligence. Their research supports the notion that children who read a lot will enhance their verbal intelligence. In other words, reading makes you smarter!

Everyone Benefits, but Struggling Readers Benefit Most

We know that early success at reading is one of the keys to developing the reading habit. However, it is the PRACTICE of the reading habit that serves to develop reading comprehension abilities (Juel, 1988; Snow, Barnes, Chandler, Goodman, & Hemphill, 1991; Stanovich, 1993). Time spent reading yields dividends for everyone—not just the good readers or smart kids. Everyone benefits from time spent reading, but struggling readers benefit the most. Struggling readers with limited reading and comprehension skills will increase vocabulary and comprehension skills when time spent reading is increased (Cunningham & Stanovich, 1998). In Four-Blocks classrooms, the Self-Selected Reading Block is designed to provide students with the practice and experience that is needed to increase reading proficiency. The research finding of Cunningham and Stanovich (1998) that reading practice benefits both the good reader and the struggling reader supports the multilevel aspect of Self-Selected Reading.

Self-Selected Reading Builds Motivation to Read

What can teachers do to help students develop intrinsic motivation to read and the reading habit? Elementary students were asked to give advice to teachers about what they should do to get their students more interested in reading.

Here are some of their suggestions:

"Teachers should let us read more."

"When we have reading time, the teacher should let us read our own books."

"Make sure you do not interrupt us while we're reading."

"Make sure there are lots of books."

These responses from children highlight the important role the teacher plays in creating a classroom environment that supports and nurtures reading motivation.

Most of us would agree that the central and most important goal of reading instruction is to foster the love of reading. Knowing how to read is not enough! Your students must have both the skill— and the will—to read. You want your students to be proficient readers who choose to read for pleasure and information. Motivation plays a critical role in reading, and it often makes the difference between reading that is rote, superficial, and shallow, and reading that is meaningful, deep, and internalized.

Reading research in the 1980's emphasized cognitive aspects of reading such as prior knowledge and strategic reading behaviors (Anderson & Pearson, 1984; Pressley, Borkowski, & Schneider, 1987). Researchers in the 1990's began to focus on a more balanced view of reading that included an emphasis on motivation and social interaction, as well as cognition and knowledge acquisition (Turner & Paris, 1995).

There are important links between motivation to read and reading achievement. For example, we know that children who are motivated to read and who spend more time reading are better readers (Taylor, Frye, & Maruyama, 1990). We know that some children come to school with a great deal more of experience with print, books, book language, and home support for reading than do other children (Allington, 1991). Perhaps most important of all, we know that supporting and nurturing reading motivation and achievement is critical to improving the education of children who find learning to read difficult (Allington, 1986; Smith-Burke, 1989).

Research suggests that spending time engaged in Self-Selected Reading promotes more positive attitudes toward reading. Wiesendanger and Birlem (1984) analyzed eleven research studies on Self-Selected Reading and reported that nine of these studies presented evidence that students develop more positive attitudes as a result of participating in Self-Selected Reading. Increases in positive attitudes toward reading have also been found for a range of students who engage in Self-Selected Reading, including remedial readers (Mayes, 1982) and adolescent students with discipline problems (Coley, 1981). These studies also suggest that an improved attitude is linked to spending more time reading, thereby helping students gain much needed practice.

Classrooms That Foster Reading Motivation and Engagement with Text

Current theory and research suggest that there are five critical classroom features that support the development of intrinsic motivation to read: book access, choice, collaboration, familiarity, and appropriate reading-related incentives. In Four-Blocks classrooms, these features are the foundation for Self-Selected Reading.

Book Access

There is abundant research that supports the notion that when children have lots of books and reading materials available, motivation to read is high (Allington & McGill-Franzen, 1991; Elley, 1992; Gambrell, 1993; Neuman & Celano, 2001). Increasing the number and range of books available to children can have a positive effect on the amount and quality of the reading experiences taking place in the classroom. Access to lots of books and reading materials is a significant factor in promoting literacy development, and attention should be devoted to assuring that high-quality classroom libraries are a priority in our schools.

While we know that having a book-rich classroom environment is essential for supporting reading development, it alone is not sufficient for the development of highly-motivated readers. It is what is done with the books that makes a difference. This "piano" analogy makes the point. Having a piano in the home will not necessarily make a child a pianist, just as having books available will not guarantee that a child will be a motivated reader. On the other hand, a pianist must have a piano to perform, and children must have books and other reading materials available to support them in becoming motivated and engaged readers. The same applies to exercise equipment. Buying the latest "abdominizer" won't have any effect on your waist size if is sits there, collecting dust and taunting you!

In the previous chapter, you were provided with lots of suggestions for obtaining, organizing, and displaying books. No classroom ever has enough books or enough space, but maximizing what you have will increase your students' access to books—and thus, their motivation to read!

Choice

The role of choice in motivation is well-recognized. Task engagement increases when students are provided with opportunities to make choices about their literacy learning. Julienne Turner (1995) observed first-grade classrooms to investigate what motivated children to engage in independent reading. She found that giving children opportunities to choose what books and materials they wanted to read resulted in increased time spent reading. In another study, students in grades 1, 3, and 5 were individually interviewed on two separate occasions (Palmer, Codling, & Gambrell, 1994). First, they were interviewed to talk about their reading of fiction; and second, to talk about reading informational text. They were asked to tell about a fiction book and a nonfiction book that they had independently read and really enjoyed. Interestingly, these students, across all grade levels, rarely mentioned books or materials that were associated with reading instruction. Rather, they overwhelmingly talked about reading materials they had chosen from the classroom library. Some students mentioned books from the school library, and a few talked about books from the home or the community library. These findings reveal that choice is strongly related to motivation, and they point out how important the classroom library is in the literacy lives of your students.

Motivation is enhanced when children choose books and reading materials for their own reasons and purposes. The power of choice is seen in the following example. If a child is told that she must clean up her messy room, the typical reaction is often not a positive one. On the other hand, if the child is presented with a number of things that must be done in order to tidy up the room and is given a choice about which job to do, the outcome is very different. For example, a parent might say, "To clean up the room, there are three jobs to do: 1. Put away stuffed animals, 2. Put games and game pieces together in their boxes, and 3. Put other toys in the toy chest. Which job would you like to do?" In this situation, instead of having a negative reaction, the child is more likely to contemplate the options, "Which job could I do quickly? Which job is the easiest? Which job would I most enjoy doing?" In such a situation where choice is provided, the child is already 'engaged' in the activity as he or she contemplates the options and is more likely to enter into the activity in a positive frame of mind. The same is true for selecting reading material. When children make choices about their reading materials, they become more engaged and motivated during the process. People of all ages are more motivated when they have some control over what they do and how they do it. Indeed, there is substantial evidence that suggests a strong correlation between choice and the development of intrinsic motivation to read (Gambrell, 1996; Paris & Oka, 1986; Turner & Paris, 1995).

Teachers can play an important role in helping children choose appropriate books and reading materials for Self-Selected Reading. If a child is choosing books that are too difficult or too easy, try using "bounded choice." Bounded choice means that the teacher provides the bounds for the choice, but the child makes the final decision about what to read. For a child who is consistently choosing books that are too difficult, the teacher might select 3 or 4 books on a topic of interest to the child that are at the appropriate level. The teacher then approaches the child with these selections, "I know you like spiders, and I found these four books I thought you might like. Would you like to have one of these for Self-Selected Reading time?" This same approach can be used with children who consistently choose books that are far too easy and provide no challenge. Chapters 6 and 7 of this text make specific suggestions for enticing children into reading books they will enjoy and can read at "just the right level."

Talking about Books
Sharing ideas and talking with others about books is an important factor in developing engaged and motivated readers. There is ample evidence that social interactions about what one has read has a positive influence on reading motivation and achievement. Self-Selected Reading is the backdrop for providing children with many opportunities to talk about books and ideas that are of great interest. Children frequently comment that have chosen a book because someone told them about it. The more books children know about, the more books they are likely to read.

Current theories of motivation and reading emphasize that learning is facilitated by social interactions with others (McCombs, 1989; Oldfather, 1993). A number of studies have documented that social interaction promotes achievement, higher-level cognition, and intrinsic desire to read (Almasi, 1995; Guthrie, Schafer, Wang, & Afflerbach, 1995). These studies found that students who engage in frequent discussions about reading with friends and family are more motivated to read and have higher reading achievement scores than do students who do not have such interactions (Campbell, et al., 2000).

In Self-Selected Reading, there are two regular opportunities for children to talk about books. Each week, teachers hold individual conferences with children. Chapter 7 will provide you with ideas for turning these conferences into "conversations" rather than "interrogations." In Chapter 8, you will find suggestions for organizing daily or weekly sharing sessions in which children talk about books with each other.

Familiarity and Curiosity
Children choose books and materials that are familiar and reflect their interests. Studies have documented that interest fosters depth of processing and enhances learning (Alexander, Kulkowich, & Hetton, 1994; Hidi, 1990). Evidence from these studies indicates that children want to read and are curious about books that are somewhat familiar. Children become familiar with books in a variety of ways, such as when friends tell them about books, when teachers tell them about books, when they have read books by the same author, and when they peruse books in libraries and bookstores.

Curiosity is also a motivator, but you can't be curious about a topic you know absolutely nothing about. Also, if you know too much about a topic you may have nothing left to be curious about. An old story, frequently told in schools to make this point, tells about a teacher who was really into her teaching. Her class was studying animals from cold climates. She read *Mr. Popper's Penguins* by by Richard and Florence Atwater aloud to her class, and they enjoyed it so much that she located all the other books in the library on penguins. After reading the ninth book aloud on penguins, she asked the class, "How did you like this book?" One child responded, "That was more than I ever wanted to know about penguins!" The point to remember is that familiarity is related to motivation, but too much information can kill curiosity. We are often motivated because we know a "little bit" about a book—we know it is a good mystery, or we have read other books by the author. If someone has told us more than we wanted to know, it may kill our curiosity and motivation to read the book ourselves.

Curiosity is acknowledged to be a driving force in motivation, and it seems important to emphasize that children are curious about and more motivated to read books that are familiar to them. In order for children to be interested and curious about books, there must be a systematic approach to book sharing.

What About Rewards?
As teachers, we would like for all of our students to find reading personally rewarding. Our hope is that our students will choose to read when no one is looking, when no one is offering a reward. We hope that they will choose to read for the spontaneous experience of enjoyment, interest, and satisfaction that comes from engagement with books and other reading materials.

If we want to create a classroom climate that supports the desire to read, it is important to think about intrinsic and extrinsic motivation. When a person is intrinsically motivated, they engage in an activity, like reading, because they want to do it. But, if a person engages in an activity only because they will receive a reward, we say that person is extrinsically motivated. Extrinsically motivated behaviors are done for external incentives or consequences. Here is an example of an external incentive, "You will receive a piece of candy for every book you read." And here is an example of an external consequence, "You read that book, so here is a piece of candy for you." An external incentive is a promise of a reward if a certain behavior is exhibited, and external consequence is a reward given for a certain behavior. Intrinsically motivated behaviors are done for the personal enjoyment and satisfaction. I think we would all agree that we want our students to be intrinsically motivated to read—for the joy and knowledge gained from reading.

Should we use rewards to encourage children to read? How do rewards affect intrinsic motivation? These are complex questions that are worth thinking about (see Gambrell and Marinak, 1997, for an in-depth discussion on developing the intrinsic desire to read). In spite of the research that suggests the negative effects of rewards, the use of rewards to entice children to read, such as gold stars, candy, and tokens, is fairly common. Fawson and Fawson (1994) investigated a program that offered elementary children an incentive (a popular food) for reading a certain number of books. When they compared the experimental incentive group with the control group, they found that intrinsic motivation to read did not increase as a result of the incentive program. The concern about using extrinsic rewards is that they may have a detrimental effect on the intrinsic motivation to read. Some researchers have suggested that if a child who enjoys reading is externally reinforced with incentives such as points, food, or money, the child may choose to read less frequently once the incentive is discontinued (Deci, Valerand, Pelletier & Ryan, 1991).

On the other hand, an analysis of the research on rewards and incentives found that rewards do not necessarily have a negative impact on intrinsic motivation with respect to attitude, time on task, and performance (Cameron & Pierce, 1994). These findings run counter to views expressed by many educators and psychologists and point to the complex nature of the relationship between incentives and motivation.

A number of studies have shown that, under certain conditions, rewards can enhance motivation. In these studies, students who were given an incentive (promised a reward for certain behavior) showed an increase in intrinsic motivation compared to students who were not offered an incentive (Brennan & Glover, 1980; Karnoil & Ross, 1977). Other researchers, however, have reported a negative effect on intrinsic motivation when incentives were promised for a specified level of performance (Deci, 1975; Lepper, Greene, & Nisbett, 1973).

There is also evidence in the psychological literature that suggests that we are motivated by the reward itself. For example, if we are paid to do a task such as reading, it may result in a decrease in our desire to read; however, we may be more motivated to make money! In other words, we tend to view the "reward" as desirable and valuable. This suggests that if we want to develop the intrinsic desire to read, books and extra time to read are the best rewards.

If books, reading related materials, and extra time to read are used as incentives, children will tend to view the reward (books, bookmarks, time to read) as desirable and valuable. Thus, book-related extrinsic rewards can be used effectively, particularly to increase the intrinsic motivation of children who do not have a literacy-rich background and who do not value books and literacy. We call this concept the "reward proximity hypothesis"—the closer the reward (books, for example) to the desired behavior (reading) the greater the likelihood that intrinsic motivation will increase (Gambrell & Marinak, 1997).

5

READING ALOUD TO CHILDREN

In a second-grade classroom in Michigan, Deb Smith begins the Self-Selected Reading Block. The children are bright-eyed and eager to hear about the three books that Deb will be sharing with them during today's teacher read-aloud session. Deb has 20 second-graders in her class, 18 of whom are on free lunch, and two who are on reduced-price lunch. Five of these children are classified as "special education students" —one autistic, one hearing impaired and learning disabled, two educational mentally impaired and ADHD, and one learning disabled child with cerebral palsy. Only two children in the class are reading on-grade-level, with the remaining 18 at the beginning stages of emergent reading. For these children, Deb knows that the teacher read-aloud session is an extremely important part of the Self-Selected Reading Block. Of the four blocks, Self-Selected Reading is Deb's favorite. Because her children have long bus rides on overcrowded buses, she begins each morning with the Self-Selected Reading Block and the teacher read-aloud. Deb believes that, after the long and noisy bus ride, the quiet, calm atmosphere of the teacher read-aloud session is a wonderful way to begin the day.

For her daily teacher read-aloud session, Deb selects three books—a chapter book, a nonfiction book, and an "everyone book." The everyone book is a simple, short (usually 8–16 pages) predictable pattern book. Deb does not call these "easy" books, instead she calls them "everyone books"—books that everyone in the class can read and enjoy. While there are dozens of creative and imaginative ways that teachers conduct teacher read-aloud sessions, Deb accomplishes several goals by beginning each session with the sharing of three different books. First, she helps children become familiar with not just one, but three books at each session! She illustrates that all kinds of good books are available for reading. Second, she highlights informational books (nonfiction) and sends the message that time spent with informational books can be fun and enjoyable. Third, with the "everyone book," she sends the message that there are some books that are just right for pleasure reading. All children want to be viewed as proficient and competent learners, and labeling books as "easy" will turn off struggling readers. By calling these books "everyone books," Deb has made them acceptable to both the proficient and less proficient readers. (Adapted from "My 'High Risk' Students Love Reading Real Books!" by Deb Smith in Cunningham & Hall's *True Stories From Four Blocks Classrooms.*)

Teacher Read-Aloud Sessions and Self-Selected Reading

In Four-Blocks® classrooms, Self-Selected Reading is the time during the day when children read materials of their own choosing. This is the block where each child develops a personal relationship with books and other reading materials. It is the time when children develop confidence, independence, skills, and an appreciation of the pleasure and knowledge that come from reading.

One important feature of the Self-Selected Reading Block is the teacher read-aloud session. Perhaps the single most important thing we can do to help children develop the knowledge required for competence in reading is to read aloud to them. Read-aloud time provides children with opportunities to hear the rich and diverse language of books, as well as the rhythm and flow of language. The specific abilities that provide the foundation for reading success come from immediate experiences with books.

During the 30-40 minutes designated for Self-Selected Reading, a portion of time is devoted to the teacher read-aloud. Early in the year, more time goes to the teacher read-aloud and to modeling and practicing routines. As children learn and get in the habit of doing the routines of Self-Selected Reading, the time for the teacher read-aloud decreases and the time for independent reading is increased. Usually, the Self-Selected Reading Block begins with the teacher read-aloud, but in some classrooms, the teacher read-aloud is the concluding activity.

Teacher read-aloud time allows children to enjoy books and stories that may be related to a topic or theme being explored in the classroom, that may be appealing to the class, but too difficult for them to read independently, or that may be special to the teacher. The teacher read-aloud is also an important motivational strategy. When children hear a good book, they often want to read it for themselves. They also may want to read other books by the same author or more about the topic. The teacher read-aloud is often the springboard that supports children in making selections about the books they will read independently during Self-Selected Reading. To make the teacher read-aloud session interesting and appealing, many different types of reading materials should be read aloud, including fiction, nonfiction, and poetry. Also, there are a number of different ways to conduct the teacher read-aloud, and it is equally important to add variety and spice to the daily read-aloud sessions.

The "Teacher Blessing of the Books" Phenomenon

"I can't wait to get my hands on that book," whispered Germaine. He was sitting on the carpet with the rest of his class as the teacher finished reading *Dinosaur Detectives* by Peter Crisp. In another classroom, the teacher holds up several books and tells "just a little bit" about each one. She talks about how she "loves" all the books by one of the authors. She reads just a page or two from another book and shows a few of the illustrations. Then, the teacher tells her students that she will put these books in some of the book crates—and that they might like to try one of these books. Later that day, she notices that all of those books are being read by children during Self-Selected Reading.

One of the most effective ways to motivate students to read is the simple teacher read-aloud session. When teachers read books and materials aloud to the class, the children are eager to get their hands on those books—the books that the teacher has "blessed." The books that teachers read aloud become special to children; they are the books that are the most sought after, and the ones that are remembered for years to come. The more books that you bless, the more books your students are going to be motivated to read!

In 1975, Sterl Artley asked college students this question, "What did your teachers (on any level) do that you feel prompted your competence and interest in reading?" The majority of students responded that teachers reading aloud to the class was what got them most interested in reading. In some cases, they reported that the teacher read the opening chapter of a book or just an interesting episode from it as a starter. Other teachers, they remembered, read a complete book, chapter by chapter. These books were usually a step or two above the reading level of the majority of the class. Some students reported that their teachers frequently talked to the class about good books, and some teachers talked about adult books they were reading for pleasure or information. From this study, it is clear that we remember pleasant and enjoyable experiences with books and that the teacher read-aloud is an excellent motivational technique for encouraging independent reading.

Recently, other researchers have asked elementary children about what motivates them to read particular books (Palmer, Codling, & Gambrell, 1994). One of the most frequently occurring responses from children is, "My teacher read it to the class," or "My teacher read part of this book aloud." Because the teacher read-aloud is a powerful motivational tool, it makes sense that it should be an important part of Self-Selected Reading.

Although there are a variety of ways to conduct teacher read-aloud sessions, there are some basics that are worth considering. The choice and variety of books is important. You must read aloud effectively, create a comfortable atmosphere, and support student's responses to what you have read aloud. There are many ingredients to the effective teacher read-aloud session.

Choosing Just the Right Books for the Read-Aloud

You want to motivate your students to read and enjoy a wide range of books and materials. The teacher read-aloud for one day might be an article from *Time* magazine about black bears, the next day it might be a short folk tale, and the third day, it might be a chapter from a book that will take several days to complete. Be sure you choose books and materials that both you and your students will enjoy. The children will know if you are not interested in what you are reading. Choose books that will challenge your student's imaginations, inspire them to dream, and make them laugh, cry, and beg for more books! Enthusiasm for reading is contagious. A teachers who loves reading will have students who love reading.

Reading "One-Sit" and "Chapter" Books Aloud
In the primary grades, some teachers almost always read books that are short and can be read in one sitting. We call these books "one-sit books." Teachers in the upper grades often read only chapter books to their students. Regardless of the grade level you teach, it is important that your students be exposed to both "one-sit books" and "chapter books." You want kindergarten and first-grade children to learn that some books take longer to read than others. And, you want older students to know that there are excellent books that take only minutes to read.

With longer books appropriate for kindergarten and first grade, you can break them into two sections to be shared across two days. You also want older students to know and appreciate some books that are short (one-sit books) but carry a powerful message. Several of Eve Bunting's books are excellent examples of one-sit books that are appropriate for reading aloud to children from kindergarten through the upper elementary grades. In *Fly Away Home*, a book that can easily be read in one sitting, she tells the story of a homeless family that lives in an airport. This is a book that kindergartners, as well as fifth- and sixth-graders, find compelling.

Bag of Books
The Bag of Books technique can be used once a week, or just occasionally, for the teacher read-aloud. This technique provides variety and promotes self-selection of high-quality literature. The theory behind this very practical strategy is based on the "teacher blessing of the book" phenomenon. The Bag of Books technique lets you bless a lot of books in 10–15 minutes. Here is how it works. Instead of reading a one-sit book or a book chapter for the teacher read-aloud session, you collect about 8 to 12 books that you think will appeal to your students. Some should be easy enough for the most struggling reader in the class, and some should challenge even the most proficient reader. You will want to include a range of informational books, some poetry, some fiction, and perhaps some magazine and

newspaper articles. The idea is to gather the children together for the teacher read-aloud time and tell them that you have a whole bag of books to share with them. Then, proceed to introduce the books briefly, giving the title and author, and perhaps commenting on the topic, cover illustration, or author as you tell about or read "just a little bit" from each book. You might read just the first paragraph, or if you have read the book yourself, you might tell "just a bit about it." (It is not necessary that you read all these books before sharing them, but you should peruse them to find something interesting to share or read aloud.) After you have introduced the books from the bag, put them on the reading table or in the book baskets and watch them disappear!

Balancing Narrative and Informational Text

There is ample research evidence that students of all ages, from elementary to high school, have difficulty comprehending informational or expository text. Some literacy authorities have specu-lated that the root of the problem is that young children lack adequate exposure to informational text, particularly in the elementary grades where narrative or fiction predominates. Nell Duke (2000) investigated the degree to which informational texts were actually included in first-grade class-rooms. She looked at the types of books in the classroom library, as well as the types of text on the classroom walls. She found that few, if any, informational texts were included in the classroom libraries, very little informational text displayed on the classroom walls, and children spent an average of only 3.6 minutes across the entire school day on experiences with informational texts! Perhaps the most telling finding from Duke's research was the scarcity of the use of informational text for children in classrooms in low socioeconomic schools. In over half of these classrooms, children spent no time at all with informational texts. This research suggests that many children lack adequate exposure to informational text, yet such exposure is necessary for building the famil-iarity, comfort, and confidence needed for learning to read informational text. In Four-Blocks class-rooms, teachers try to read aloud equal amounts of narrative and informational text so that children have adequate and appropriate experiences with both genres.

Achieving a Good Balance—Some Suggested Books

To illustrate a good balance of reading materials, this section includes some brief lists of great books for teacher read-aloud sessions. The books are loosely divided into three categories: books for younger readers, older readers, and books for everyone. In each of these categories, you will find some fiction, nonfiction, and some poetry. You will also find in each category some one-sit books and some longer books that can be read as chapter books. In the list of read-aloud books for younger readers, you will find wordless picture books, pattern books, rhyming books, and some books that have sophisticated language and story structures. The list of read-aloud books for older readers also has books that are shorter and easier to read, as well as some that are longer and more complex. The topics in this category are those that older readers find more appealing. In the section, of read-aloud books for all ages, you will find one-sit books and a few chapter books that will be interesting and enjoyable to read aloud to students of any age. Some of these books are silly (*The Dumb Bunnies*) and some deal with serious and thoughtful issues (*Fly Away Home*). What all of these books have in common is that they are great books for reading aloud.

Teacher Read-Aloud Books for Younger Readers

Miss Nelson Is Missing by Harry Allard

Finding Providence: The Story of Roger Williams by Avi

Chicken Socks by Brod Bogert

The Very Hungry Caterpillar by Eric Carle

Guess Who's Coming, Jesse Bear by Joy Cowley

In the Tall, Tall Grass by Denise Fleming

Eruption! The Story of Volcanoes by Anita Ganeri

Tool Book by Gail Gibbons

Shrewbetinna's Birthday by John Goodall (wordless picture book)

Tell Me a Story, Mama by Angela Johnson

The Creepy Thing by Fernando Krahn (wordless picture book)

Eating Fractions by Bruce McMillan

Brown Bear, Brown Bear, What Do You See? by Bill Martin, Jr.

Frog on His Own by Mercer Mayer (wordless picture book)

Back Home by Gloria Jean Pinkney

Alexander and the Terrible, Horrible, No Good, Very Bad Day by Judith Viorst

Teacher Read-Aloud Books for Older Readers

Dinosaur Detectives by Peter Crisp

Dear Mr. Henshaw by Beverly Cleary

Because of Winn-Dixie by Kate DiCamillo

No More Homework! No More Texts!: Kids Favorite Funny School Poems
    by Bruce Lansky

The Lion, the Witch, and the Wardrobe by C.S. Lewis

Sarah, Plain and Tall by Patricia MacLachlan

Fast Sam, Cool Clyde and Stuff by Walter Dean Myers

Favorite Greek Myths by Mary Pope Osborne

Dogsong by Gary Paterson

Rosa Parks: My Story by Rosa Parks (with James Haskins)

Bridge to Terabithia by Katherine Paterson

New Kid on the Block by Jack Prelutsky

Ruby the Copycat by Peggy Rathmann

The Little Prince by Antoine Saint-Exupery

Maniac Magee by Jerry Spinelli

Faithful Elephants by Yukio Tsuchiya

Trumpet of the Swan by E. B. White

Teacher Read-Aloud Books for All Ages

Fly Away Home by Eve Bunting
The Wall by Eve Bunting
The Fourth Little Pig by Theresa Celsi
The Dumb Bunnies by Sue Denim
Oh, How I Wished I Could Read by John Gile
Something for Nothing by Phoebe Gillman
Shelia Rae, the Brave by Kevin Henkes
My Great Aunt Arizona by Gloria Houston
I'll Love You Forever by Robert Munch
The Giving Tree by Shel Silverstein
Chato's Kitchen by Gary Soto
Mufaro's Beautiful Daughter by John Steptoe
Alexander and the Terrible, Horrible, No Good, Very Bad Day by Judith Viorst
Charlotte's Web by E. B. White
The Velveteen Rabbit by Margery Williams
The Memory Coat by Elvira Woodruff

Tips for Effective and Exciting Read-Alouds

Get Familiar with the Books You Will Read Aloud

While it is not always necessary to read every word of a book or the material you choose for the teacher read-aloud session, it is a good idea to spend a few minutes getting "comfortable" with the text. Read the first page or two, and then survey the book. Get a feel for the kind of dialogue or information that is conveyed in the book. As you do this, think about whether this is a book that you can effectively read aloud, or whether this is a book that will need more careful preparation. Not all books need to be read completely before you read them aloud, but some need more preparation than others. The bottom line is that you want the read-aloud session to be both interesting and effective, and spending just a little time with the book prior to the read-aloud session will help you do just that.

Create a Comfortable and Inviting Climate

You send a clear message to your students that reading is important by taking the time to read to them daily. It is very important to set aside a specific time during Self-Selected Reading for the teacher read-aloud, rather than trying to fit it into the schedule haphazardly.

Make read-aloud time special and inviting. In some classrooms, teachers set up a special corner for read-aloud time with a rocking chair and rug. In other classrooms, teachers move around the room, showing the illustrations to the children as they move from one table of children to the other.

Introduce the book with a few comments. Tell something about the book or the author or why you chose the book to read aloud. You might even introduce the book by saying, "I liked the picture on the cover of this book, but I haven't had time to read it yet. I'd like to know what you think of it." Point out interesting or unusual end pages, title pages, and dedication pages so that children learn these features of books. With informational books, take a few minutes to show the table of contents, glossary, index, or other features, such as the use of headings, charts, and maps.

Rituals can also make read-aloud time special. For example, students can nominate a book to be read aloud by the teacher by putting a card with the title and the author's name in a box or goldfish bowl, along with a comment about why they think it is a good book for the teacher read-aloud. The teacher can then draw from the fishbowl to select some of the books to be used for the read-aloud session. One third-grade child nominated *Aunt Isabel Tells a Good One* by Kate Duke and wrote, "This is a good story about a good story." In a second-grade classroom, a child nominated *Rain Makes Applesauce* by Julian Scheer with the comment, "This book is better than sliced bread!" Children who have nominated books that are randomly selected will enjoy helping you to introduce "their" book by giving the title and the author and telling why they think it is a great book for read-aloud.

In another classroom, the teacher and the children have a Friday ritual. During the teacher read-aloud every Friday, the children have popcorn. Another teacher frequently brings in an object that is related to the story. For example, when he read *Something for Nothing* by Phoebe Gillman, a story about a grandfather who makes a blanket for his grandson, the teacher brought in a pin cushion. He asked the children "What is this, and who would use it?" This was a wonderful way to introduce this story about a tailor to the children.

Self-Selected Reading The Four-Blocks® Way

With younger and less proficient readers, particularly in kindergarten and first grade, the attention span of the students is an important consideration. You might want to schedule two or three shorter read-aloud sessions, instead of one longer one, especially at the beginning of the year. One session might be conducted at another time of the day and then one at the beginning of Self-Selected Reading. If this seems to be a good idea for your students, think about doing book-links. Book-links have a related theme, common author, or "tie-in." For example, during the first read-aloud you might read *Zoe's Webs* by Thomas West, a very short and delightful story about a baby spider learning to weave webs. For the second read-aloud period, you might choose to read a short informational book about spiders. Children will enjoy responding to questions that foster comparisons such as: What was the most important thing you learned about spiders? How were these two books alike? How were they different?

For an author book-link, you might choose Eric Carle's *The Very Hungry Caterpillar* for the first session and another Eric Carle book for the second session. Children will enjoy comparing and contrasting books by the same author as they respond to questions like, "How are the two books similar? How would you describe books by Eric Carle? Which is your favorite and why?" As children develop more extended attention spans and listening skills, the read-aloud session can gradually lengthen.

Read the Selection with Interest and Feeling
Let your voice convey the mood or tone of the text. If you are reading fiction, let your voice show excitement, enthusiasm, or sadness. Use different "voices" for different characters. If you are reading a book that has a predictable pattern, let the students help you "read" the text by chiming in with the predictable refrain. If you are reading nonfiction, emphasize the really important or exciting parts of the text; show your interest and enthusiasm for real world knowledge. Comment on new or interesting information or words as you read.

Timing is also an important feature of an effective teacher read-aloud. Make effective use of timing as you read aloud by pausing at the high-point of a story to give students time to digest and contemplate what has happened. This gives students time to consider the ideas conveyed in the text. Pausing right before a significant "action" in the story can heighten suspense, and encourages children to think about what might happen next.

Vary your approach to reading aloud. Some books should be read aloud straight through, without any interruption or comment from either you or the children. Other books are just perfect for inviting responses throughout the reading.

Highlight Interesting Language and the Meanings of Unfamiliar Words
Our richest and most interesting vocabulary is found in books. In our everyday conversations, we most often use our "comfort" language. For example, if you were talking about a favorite aunt, you might say, "Aunt Alice is always happy," rather than "Aunt Alice is full of zest." In books we find wonderfully rich language that children will not be exposed to unless someone reads to them on a consistent basis.

As you read books that have rhythm and well-turned phrases that are appealing to the ear, repeat the lines and tell your students why you like those lines or phrases. Highlight language techniques and interesting language patterns that authors use to make some stories so wonderful to listen to and read. Sometimes it is best to finish reading the story and then go back and highlight these features. Use sticky notes to mark these places so you can quickly locate them when you finish reading the story aloud.

Read-aloud time provides great opportunities to help students develop an understanding of rare and unusual new words. As you come across words that might be unfamiliar to children during the teacher read-aloud, briefly comment and give some insight into the word meaning. ("Rude—what an interesting word to describe a cat. I guess he's not always nice to the other cats!") Be cautious about disrupting the story too often for this purpose. You don't want to overdo this, as it can destroy interest in the story or information. Sometimes it is better to read to the end of the sentence or even the end of the paragraph and then go back to comment on a rare or unusual word.

Inviting Children's Responses

Children like to talk about the books that teachers read aloud. A study conducted by Mendoza (1985) revealed that many teachers do not discuss books that they read aloud with their students. Yet, in talking with children, Mendoza found that over 70% reported that they wanted to talk about the books the teacher read aloud. It appears that we make a mistake by thinking that once we have read a book aloud to students, that should be the end of it. During and after the teacher read-aloud, be sure to give children an opportunity to respond to what you have read. This step can be accomplished in a brief discussion of the student's reactions. ("What did you think of that story?" "What was your favorite part of the story?" "What was the most important thing you learned about _____?") You can also use the Partner Quickshare technique (described on page 96) and have the children turn to a partner and talk for one minute each, using the following prompts:

"What did you like best about this book?"

"What was the most interesting thing you learned about _____(give the topic)?"

"What else would you like to know about _____ (give the topic)?"

This technique is time-efficient, yet it allows children to think about and respond to the story or informational text in a personal way.

Inviting children to talk about the book you are reading aloud helps them develop a strong comprehension of the text (Barrentine, 1996). Some ways to do this include:

- Invite them to make predictions.

  "What do you think George will do next?"

  Don't forget to talk about whether their predictions were confirmed or disproved.

- Invite children to make connections to other books.

  "Do you remember another story we read about bears? How are the stories alike? How were they different?"

- Invite children to make personal connections.

  "Have you ever had to make a really difficult decision like the character in this book?"

- Ask children about character attributes:

  "How would you describe _____?"

  "What do you think made _____ behave that way?"

  "How would you describe _____ at the beginning of the story?...at the end of the story? What do you think makes _____ tick?"

You will certainly NOT want to do all of these things with every book. If you did, there would be little, if any, time left for reading aloud! Remember that reading to students should take most of your teacher read-aloud time, but do take some time to think about the unique qualities of the books you read aloud and invite children's responses.

As children respond to the books you are reading aloud, be accepting of all of their ideas and value their contributions. When children make insightful or interesting comments, follow-up by asking questions such as, "What made you think that?" or "What clues did the author give to make you think that?"

It is important that we strive to understand the thinking behind the ideas that children express. Be a good model and ask questions to which you do not know the answer. If you find the answer to your question as the story unfolds, let children in on it by saying something like, "Oh, now I see why...."

At the conclusion of the read-aloud, it is always a good idea to mention other books by the same author and/or other books on the same topic. If possible, have copies of these books to add to the book crates for Self-Selected Reading.

Making the Teacher Read-Aloud Selections Available to Students
Almost all children want to get their hands on the teacher read-aloud book! They like to look more closely at the illustrations, and many students will want to read the book on their own. You can make the teacher read-aloud selections more available to students in a variety of ways.

- Place the teacher read-aloud book in the crates used for Self-Selected Reading.

- Get multiple copies of the book, perhaps from the school library, and place copies in several of the book crates.

- Have a special table or spot in the classroom where teacher read-aloud books are featured.

- Set up a listening corner featuring the teacher read-aloud book on an audiotape so children can "hear it again" as they follow along in the book.

- Post a chart in the classroom that lists the titles and authors of all the teacher read-aloud selections throughout the year.

- Let children who want to read the book put their names in a special bowl or container. Draw names to make an ordered list of who gets the book next.

Adding Variety and Spice to the Teacher Read-Aloud Session

The most important components of a teacher read-aloud session have already been discussed.

- Choose from a variety of books.
- Prepare for your reading.
- Make the read-aloud an enjoyable experience.
- Invite responses and book talk from the children.

Once these are in place, you may want to add some variety and spice to your teacher read-alouds. Here are some possibilities:

Guest Readers
Invite parents, grandparents, the librarian, principal, reading teachers, and others to read aloud a favorite book to the class. Each person will bring a unique style to the presentation of their favorite read-aloud book. Be sure to ask each guest reader to tell a little bit about why the book is a favorite.

Class "Best Seller" List
Keep a class chart of all the books you read aloud to the class. At the end of each month, have the students vote on their favorite short storybook, chapter book, informational book, or perhaps their favorite illustrations. Children enjoy voting on their favorites, and you can engage them in tallying the results. Stars or blue ribbons can be placed on the classroom chart beside the favorite titles. Also, you can have children vote on the book they would most like to have read aloud again by the teacher—and then have a special day and time when you read that favorite again.

Include High-Quality Multicultural Literature

Reading and sharing books about many different cultures can help children understand and appreciate them. For example, a first-grade teacher read *Tortillas* by Margarita Gonzalez-Jensen aloud to the class at the beginning of the Self-Selected Reading Block. This is a delightful pattern book about eating tortillas. ("Tortillas, tortillas. We eat crisp ones and soft ones. Tortillas, Tortillas. We eat them in a bowl with milk.") The book also has warm, wonderful illustrations by Rene King Moreno of a family eating tortillas with a variety of fillings. At the conclusion of the read-aloud, the teacher invited children's responses by asking, "How many of you have ever eaten a tortilla?" Only a few children responded that they had even eaten one. The teacher then asked, "If you were going to eat a tortilla, what do you think you would like to put on it?" Responses were tabulated, and the favorite toppings were identified. The next day, the teacher brought in tortillas with lots of favorite toppings or fillings (powdered sugar, sour cream, lettuce, chopped tomatoes, honey, etc.). Each child chose one or two toppings for his tortilla. While the children ate their tortillas, the teacher reread *Tortillas* aloud. Later, the children did patterned writing by completing the following frame:

Tortilla, tortilla. I like my tortillas with _____.

The children drew pictures of their tortillas, and then all the work was collected into a class book titled "Room 10 Eats Tortillas."

Fortunately, there are many wonderful multicultural books that we can share with our students. According to Harris (1992), multicultural literature focuses on minority cultures, regional cultures, religious minorities, people with exceptionalities, the aged, and literature that describes women in non-stereotypical roles. High-quality multicultural literature accurately represents the group's values, history, and language and avoids stereotyped characters. When we share multicultural literature during the read-aloud session, we help our students understand and value the unique nature of other cultures.

Really Great Resources: Finding Books for the Teacher Read-Aloud

It's easy to find good books to read aloud to students. Today, we have so many resources available to help us find those books that make special read-aloud books. Here are some suggestions:

Ask Your Students for Recommendations

Your students know books that they especially love and want to hear over and over again. This is important because research by Elley (1989) suggests that it takes more than one read-aloud of a book to make a difference in a child's vocabulary development. In other words, children do not internalize new vocabulary from hearing a book read once, but by the third reading of a book it is likely that they will have internalized a number of new words and their meanings. Promote the idea that there are many books that we want to hear over and over again. Encourage your students to recommend books for the teacher read-aloud; you might even want to make a list of these recommendations.

Newbery Medal Books

The Newbery Medal, awarded annually since 1952, is presented to an author in recognition of the most distinguished contribution to American literature for children during the previous year. This list of award-winning books (see pages 130-144) includes some that you will surely want to read aloud to your students. You will want to introduce your students to some other books on the list by reading an introductory paragraph or a section that describes an exciting event. While these award-winning books are selected by adults and meet the highest standards of good literature, it is important to remember that not all of these books will appeal to or be appropriate for your students. Select wisely to share this good literature with your students. You'll even find some of your favorites on this list!

Caldecott Medal Books

The Caldecott Medal, awarded annually since 1938, is presented to an illustrator in recognition of the most distinguished picture book for children published in the United States during the previous year. You will find many books on this list (see pages 117-128) that you will want to read-aloud and share with your students. Your students will enjoy studying and comparing the different styles of the illustrators and discussing how the illustrations convey the mood, feeling, and messages of a particular text.

Children's Literature Internet Sites

KIDLIT-L is an internet mailing list that provides wonderful information about children's literature. Subscribers to this mailing list share ideas and insights about good literature. You can subscribe to this list by sending a request to the administrative address listed below.
Address: listserv@bingvmb.cc.binghamton.edu

The Children's Literature Web Guide is a central site for children's literature. Here you will find an extensive set of links to a wide range of children's literature resources.
Address: http:///www.ucalgary.ca/~dkbrown/indes.html

The Reading Zone of the Internet Public Library is another central site for children's literature. You will want to explore this site with links to literature resources.
Address: http://ww.ipl.org/youth/lapage.html

Children's Choices

Children from all across the country participate in the process of selecting good books to be listed as "Children's Choices." The children read and vote on their favorites books. Sponsored by the International Reading Association (IRA) and the Children's Book Council, this list of good books appears annually in the October issue of *The Reading Teacher*. A free copy of the most recent choices will be mailed to you if you send a self-addressed 9 x 12-inch envelope, stamped with first-class postage (2 oz. weight), to IRA, P. O. Box 8139, Newark, DE 19714.

Teacher's Choices

Teachers from across the country read and vote on their choices of good literature. The process for identifying Teacher's Choices is similar to Children's Choices and is also sponsored by the IRA and the Children's Book Council. You can receive a copy of the most recent Teacher's Choices list by following the same procedure as described above and mailing your request to the same IRA address.

Read Children's Literature

All of the above resources will provide you with good information about the wealth of good literature available for young children. None of these, however can take the place of reading children's literature on a regular basis. The more you read and enjoy children's literature yourself, the more you will enjoy reading to your students. As you develop your repertoire of favorites, you will find that you are better able to make appropriate choices about selections for teacher read-aloud sessions, titles to include in the classroom library, and special books to recommend to the children in your classroom.

Teacher Read-Aloud: An Essential Part of Self-Selected Reading

Teacher read-aloud sessions are an essential part of Self-Selected Reading. The literature that is read aloud to children fosters high-level thinking skills, increases world knowledge, enhances multicultural understanding, and promotes the simple pleasure of reading.

Perhaps one of the most important aspects of the teacher read-aloud session is that it fosters children's motivation to read. Hearing good books read aloud captures children's interests and develops their desire to read independently. Second, teacher read-aloud sessions increase vocabulary knowledge as children are exposed to the rich and complex language patterns found in books. Third, read-aloud sessions help children develop an awareness of how stories and informational texts are structured. Fourth, read-aloud sessions promote student's comprehension as they are able to focus on understanding the written message and extend their background of experience.

When teachers read aloud to their students, it conveys the message that reading is important, fun, and informative. The most important goal of reading instruction in Four-Blocks classrooms is to develop independent readers—who know how to read and choose to read for pleasure and information. When children choose to read, they have increased opportunities to develop their reading abilities. Teacher read-aloud sessions provide many rich experiences that help children develop both the skill and the will to read.

6

CHILDREN READING

In Chapter 1, we took you on an imaginary journey into many different classrooms during their Self-Selected Reading time. We hope that you noticed the many and varied forms the reading takes depending on the age of the children, the constraints or possibilities of the classroom space, and the preferences of the teacher. Of course, since your imaginary visit took place in the spring, the routines and procedures for Self-Selected Reading in each classroom were already in place. Students knew what was expected of them during this time and everything went smoothly. As you might imagine, this smooth-running, quiet reading time did not happen automatically. Children learned the behaviors expected of them and what was allowed (and not allowed!) during the first weeks of school through demonstration, modeling, and practice.

Self-Selected Reading, like the other three blocks, gets 30-40 minutes each day (less time in kindergarten). Early in the year, more of this time goes to the teacher read-aloud and to modeling and practicing routines, and the actual time for children to read is shorter. As children learn and get in the habit of doing what is expected of them, the time for quiet reading and conferencing is increased gradually until it equals 15–20 minutes. This chapter will describe these variations in detail and help you decide what your classroom Self-Selected Reading time will look like and how to get it to look that way.

Where Will They Read? The "No Wandering" Rule

Where the children read is a decision you and the children make. In some classrooms, children sit at their desks or tables and read. In other classrooms, children are spread out all over the room. The most important consideration about where children read is that they must have a variety of reading materials within arms reach because during Self-Selected Reading time, a "NO WANDERING!" rule is strictly enforced. This rule was developed during our first year of doing Four-Blocks® (1989-90). We observed again and again that when children were allowed to move from place to place during the Self-Selected Reading time, the children who struggled most with reading moved a lot more than they read! These struggling readers quietly, and without disrupting others or calling attention to themselves, went from place to place, pausing for a minute or two to "turn some pages" in a book or magazine, then moving on to another spot! Halfway through first grade, they seem to have figured out a strategy for getting through the Self-Selected Reading time without doing very much reading—by keeping on the move!

Here are some of the ways teachers provide children with lots of choices for their reading without having any children moving from place to place.

Book Crates

In some Four-Blocks classrooms, you will see children reading from crates or buckets of books placed at their tables. The crates contain a "smorgasbord" of books from various genres and at different levels. Books read during the teacher read-aloud are often added to the crates after they are read, along with other books on similar topics or by the same author. Books read during Guided Reading, along with other books by the same author, are also added to the crates. Children like reading the books they have heard the teacher read, and rereading favorite stories they first read during the Guided Reading Block.

When crates are used as the major way of making lots of books available within arms reach, the crates move from table to table. In kindergarten and early primary grades, it is common for the crates to move daily or weekly. As the children get older, teachers often rotate the crates each week. Most teachers designate the crates with colors or numbers and sticker each book that belongs in that crate with a matching number or color. At the end of Self-Selected Reading time, all books are returned to their crates. Some teachers remove the crates from the tables at the end of Self-Selected Reading, while other teachers leave the crates on the tables so that children can read some more as they have extra time throughout the day.

If you are going to use the crates as your major way of making lots of books easily available, you will have to solve the problem of children who are in the middle of a great book when the time for reading ends. Imagine having to put your book back into the crate and having that crate move on to another table when you are at the best part! To solve this problem, most teachers establish a "reserve shelf" somewhere in the room. Each child has one bookmark in a container on the reserve shelf. If a child wants to continue reading a "crate book" the following day, he or she can remove that book from its crate, put a personalized bookmark in it, and place it on the reserve shelf. Each child is only allowed to have one book on reserve at any one time, and the child must continue reading the book the next day or return it to its crate. Children love reserving books, and the reserve shelf adds a little extra motivation and fun to the Self-Selected Reading time.

Some teachers worry that they don't have enough books to provide each grouping of children with 30-40 books from which to choose. Hopefully, you got some good ideas from Chapter 3 on obtaining books, and providing books for the crates will not be as much of a problem as you thought it might be. It is also important to remember that children—especially young children—love reading books over and over again. In the Self-Selected Reading Block, we are trying to create for all our children the experience that many "lucky" children experienced at home. Do you remember having your own shelf of books, perhaps within arms reach of your bed? How many books did you have? Most children who have books at home don't have hundreds of books. Rather, they have 30-50 books, many of which they read again and again. When the crates of books rotate to the different tables, it is not unusual to hear a child exclaim, "Oh good, we get the blue crate. It has my favorite dinosaur book." Another child may observe, "Tomorrow, when we get the #6 crate, I am going to read *Alexander and the Terrible, Horrible, No Good Very Bad Day* again!"

In some classrooms, children help provide the books for the crates. In one second-grade classroom, a boy who loved dinosaurs brought dinosaur books from home to read during Self-Selected Reading. (Remember, the books you provide are just there to make sure there are plenty of choices within reach and to make sure there are no excuses for not reading. Children who already have the reading habit and are lucky enough to have books at home are welcome to bring them in to read during Self-Selected Reading. Reading books from the school or public library is also encouraged. The crates are there to expand the reading possibilities, not to limit them!)

During sharing time, the dinosaur-infatuated boy would share pictures and information from his dinosaur books, and before long, children started borrowing his books. While the boy was willing to share, problems developed. Children begged to be the first one to borrow his book. Children fussed if they didn't get to borrow the book. The final straw was when one of his favorite dinosaur books disappeared!

The teacher considered a "no borrowing" policy, but that would have been hard to enforce and would have gone against the spirit of Self-Selected Reading. Eventually, it was the boy who came up with the solution—a crate of his dinosaur books that rotated from table to table in addition to the other crates. With parental permission, the crate was set up. Like the other crates, if a student wanted to continue reading a dinosaur book the next day, she put her bookmark in it and put the book on the reserve shelf. (Crate books are never allowed to go into desks! Like socks in the dryer, some books that go into desks are never seen again!) In addition to the dinosaur crate, other children brought in books from home and a second crate was added which contained books that they were willing to share with others in the class.

In addition to the permanent collection of crates which contain all types of books on many different levels, many teachers add special books to go with their themes, units, holidays, or author studies. These books can be added—a few to each crate—with a brief introduction of each book explaining how it relates to the theme. Alternatively, a crate of these special books could rotate along with the other crates. The table that gets the special crate should also have one of the "smorgasbord" crates so that the principle of each child selecting the type of books he or she wants to read each day is maintained. Remember that one of the major goals of Self-Selected Reading is that children will develop their reading interests. During Self-Selected Reading, teachers read aloud a variety of books to the students and make the widest range of books available to them, but the children are allowed to choose the books they want to read. If the children choose to read books about dinosaurs, or mysteries, or Clifford books every day, then they are allowed to do so. (During Guided Reading, however, the teacher chooses what the students will read and makes sure that they learn how to read all the different genres of books on a wide variety of topics.)

Personal Libraries
Some teachers like for their students to have their own collections of reading materials from which to choose. Each child has a box or a large zippered bag which contains their chosen books. A scheduled time is set for selecting books to put in the bag or box. In early grades, the materials are often chosen daily. In upper grades, book selection might happen weekly. At the beginning of the year, more time is given to book selection, and the teacher should be available to help the children pick books they will enjoy and can read. As the year goes on, most children have "found" their particular type of book, and they can choose more independently.

Some teachers help children create "Personal Library Boxes." Magazine storage boxes (available from your local office supply store) are perfect for Library Boxes, but any box that will hold a few books will work. An index card is stapled or glued to the end of each box to show the name of the child in big, bold lettering.

The teacher might introduce the use of the Personal Library Boxes by telling students that, "Good readers always have a book or magazine that they are reading. They also know what books they want to read next. Good readers always have some things to read that are quick and easy—just in case they have a few minutes to "sneak in" some reading. Since we are all good readers, we all need to have these things in our Library Boxes."

You might want to make a chart like the one shown to remind children of the contents of their Library Boxes:

WHAT'S IN MY LIBRARY BOX?

1.   MY NOW BOOK.
     The book/material I'm reading right now.

2.   MY NEXT BOOK(S).
     The book(s) or material(s) I want to read next.

3.   MY QUICK-AND-EASY READS.
     Some things that are good, quick, easy reading—such as a book
     of poetry, or magazines with short articles (*Highlights, Ranger Rick,*
     and the *Guinness Book of World Records.*)

After the boxes are filled, the children are ready to begin using them for Self-Selected Reading. They have a range of materials to choose from in their box, so if a book is too difficult, they can read one of their "next" books. If they finish a book or a chapter and there are only a few minutes left for reading, they can pick up one of their quick-and-easy reads. Personal Library Boxes can be stored on the floor along one wall of the classroom, always with the name card visible. In many classrooms, the boxes are stored beneath the chalk board because it is often unused space.

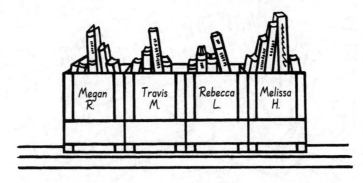

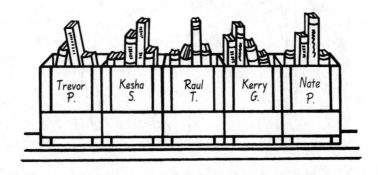

Regardless of how often selections for the library bags/boxes are made and how much guidance children are given to make good selections, the "NO WANDERING!" rule must be followed. Some teachers allow five minutes at the end of the reading time each day for children to remove and add to their libraries. Other teachers set aside a half-hour sharing/selecting time once a week. Children share their favorite books and parts of books for the week during the first 15 minutes, and then select books for the next week during the last 15 minutes.

In addition to Personal Libraries or the materials in the crates, many teachers help their students create literacy binders of materials they can easily read. The binders contain individual copies of poetry, plays, and songs previously read during Guided Reading. Some teachers duplicate copies of the class-authored books the children make and give each child a personal copy. If children get a weekly magazine, such as *Weekly Reader*, these can be collected in the binder. The binders are very popular with young children because they create a growing collection of things they can read, and they enjoy returning to these again and again throughout the year. One additional advantage of the literacy binders is that each child has a bulging collection of readable materials to take home and enjoy over the summer months.

Centers
Some classrooms have many different places where various reading materials are stored and which can be used during Self-Selected Reading. In addition to a library corner, many classrooms contain a magazine rack, a big book stash, a set of encyclopedias, and a display of student- and class-authored books. A listening center and a computer center may be available for listening to and viewing a variety of reading materials. Reading materials are often found in areas set up for science, math, and social studies explorations. In these classrooms, children can often be found reading all over the room during the Self-Selected Reading Block.

Of course, if you are going to have children reading in various centers around the room, you will need to devise a plan to make sure there are not too many people in any one area and to ensure that the "NO WANDERING!" rule is followed. You will want to designate the maximum number of students who can be in one place and develop a system for letting different children have first pick on the different centers on different days. Some teachers control the number of children who can be in each center each day by placing signs for each center on a bulletin board and letting the children place clothespins with their names on them (or some other indicator) on the center they will be in that day. If you are lucky enough to have a classroom with enough space for centers, you can spread out your reading materials and your students to make good use of centers during Self-Selected Reading. Of course, you will have to make sure that your children understand that this is READING time, and regardless of what center they are in, the only activity they can engage in is reading! For example, the computer center will be used for other activities throughout the day, but during Self-Selected Reading, it will be set up with something to read, and reading will be the only activity allowed there. The science center will be used at other times during the day for science experiments and explorations, but reading about the current science topic is the only activity allowed during Self-Selected Reading. Children who fail to follow this rule will find their clothespins (or other indicators) missing, and will lose the privilege of reading in a center for several days.

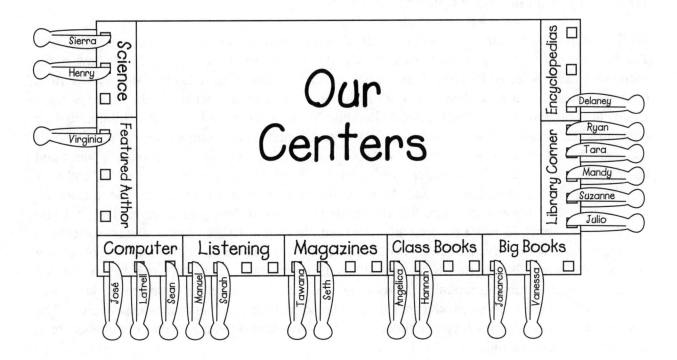

Combining Centers with Crates or Personal Libraries

Often, the best solution to where children will read is to combine crates or personal libraries and centers. Each day, let half the children choose a center to read in and the other half read at their seats from crates or Personal Libraries. On the following day, the students take turns and those who were in centers the day before are now at their seats, and vice versa. Very few classrooms have enough "spreading out" space for all the children to be reading at various places in the room, but every classroom has some good cozy places. By having half your children at their seats and half at centers, you make the best use of whatever classroom space you have, and you make all the materials in the room available for children to read during Self-Selected Reading. The children at centers are happy because they have chosen where they will be. The children at their seats have more "elbow room" because there are only half as many children at each table or in each desk grouping.

How Will They Read? By Themselves and Quietly!

The classroom during Self-Selected Reading time should be a very quiet place. Children should be reading by themselves and to themselves. Those children who still need to hear themselves reading should be reading in whisper voices. When visitors come to visit in Four-Blocks classrooms during the Self-Selected Reading Block, they often marvel at how calm and peaceful the classroom is. "Where do you get such quiet children?" they often ask.

While you may often wish you could, Four-Blocks classrooms do not get unusually quiet children! Teachers work hard during the first weeks of school to teach children the appropriate behaviors for each block. Self-Selected Reading time is quiet time, and children learn that they don't move from their spots and they read to themselves or in whisper voices. Most teachers do their teacher read-aloud at the beginning of the Self-Selected Reading Block. Then, they dismiss the children to their own individual reading time. For the first week or so, the individual reading time might only be for five minutes. The teacher spends time dismissing each table or center to their reading areas and having the rest of the children watch how quietly and quickly they get to their spots, and how quietly they choose something to read. All the children who haven't yet been dismissed from the read-aloud area observe and notice that the children already at their places are reading, but you can't "hear a word." As more children are dismissed, they tiptoe to their places and try to settle in and begin reading quickly and quietly because they know the teacher and the others are observing their Self-Selected Reading time behaviors. When the last children are settled with their books, the teacher circulates, moving around the room very quietly. She smiles, nods approval, and gives "thumbs up" signals to children who are sitting and reading to themselves or in whisper voices. The teacher stops to speak with several children, and in a very hushed voice, makes comments about their books or their reading.

"*Green Eggs and Ham* is one of my favorite books."

"You are using a wonderful whisper voice to read your book."

"Your book has some great dinosaur pictures in it. I love the picture on this page."

No more than five minutes after everyone has begun reading, the teacher calls the reading time to a close. She compliments the children on how well they did on their first day of Self-Selected Reading and shares a few pages from various books that the children have chosen, thus affirming the choices the children have made. There is time to do this at the end because the amount of time the children are sitting and reading quietly is only 5–8 minutes, depending on when they were dismissed from the large group.

The teacher continues to use this procedure of quietly dismissing different groups of children to their reading for several days or even several weeks, as long as is needed for the quiet reading time atmosphere to be established. If any child does not get quickly and quietly to a spot and begin reading, he or she is called back to the big group area and is the last to be dismissed to read, usually after a serious chat with the teacher about the importance of a quiet room so everyone can enjoy their reading.

In most classrooms, within two weeks, the dismissal to the reading speeds up considerably. The reading time can be increased gradually, a minute at a time. The teacher can spend more time having quick, whispered conversations with children about their books. Once the children can sit quietly and read for 12 minutes, the teacher can consider leaving them on their own to read as she begins to hold more formal conferences with the children.

The Self-Selected Reading Block, like the other blocks, gets 30–40 minutes each day. The amount of time that the children are reading is increased gradually throughout the year. The goal is for children to be able to read for 15–20 minutes each day. This goal can be accomplished in almost every classroom if the teacher carries out the procedures as described and increases the time for reading gradually—in one-minute intervals—until the children become accustomed to reading by themselves and quietly. Early in the year, the extra time provided by the children reading for just short periods of time is taken up with the dismissal and closure routine and with helping children learn how to choose books they can read and will enjoy.

PVC Phones and Stuffed Animals

It is hard for kindergartners and early first-graders to use whisper voices. Many teachers of young children provide them with "phones" made of PVC pipe which magnify their voices so that they can hear themselves reading even when they use quiet voices. Children love reading into these "phones." Another issue with young children reading to themselves is that many young children's only experience with reading is with someone reading aloud to them. The students feel more comfortable when they have someone to read to, so many teachers provide stuffed animals for them to read to. (Yard sales and thrift shops are a wonderful source for stuffed animals! Run them through a wash cycle before bringing them to the classroom, and wash them regularly throughout the year.)

Helping Children Choose "Just Right" Books

Many children do not know how to choose a book they will enjoy and can read. Early in the year, spend some time modeling for children how to choose a book that is "just right." If you are teaching young children, it is often helpful to read or tell them the story of Goldilocks and the Three Bears. The concept of "just right" is quickly grasped as the children delight in Papa Bear's porridge being too hot, Mama Bear's porridge being too cold, but Baby Bear's porridge being "just right." After reading and enjoying the story and talking about the "just right" porridge and chair and bed, you can relate that concept to books by telling the children that some of the books in the classroom are "just right" for them to read now. Some other books are easy, and they will enjoy reading them because they can read through them quickly. Some books are too hard right now, but as the year goes on and they become better and better readers, these "too hard" books will become "just right." Tell them that, before deciding if a book is "easy," "just right," or "too hard," they should look through it and decide if it is a book they would enjoy reading. Next, you may want to pick up several books and demonstrate how to select a book. Here is an example of what that demonstration might sound and look like:

"Boys and girls, today we are going to practice choosing books. First, we will look through the book and decide if we would like to read it. Next, I will show you how to decide if it is 'easy,' ' just right,' or 'too hard for now.' To decide if I like a book, I look at the cover and the pictures. On the cover of this book, I see a picture of a boy and a bike. It looks like a new bike, and the boy seems happy with it. Now, I am going to look at some of the pictures and think about what is happening and decide if this is a book I will probably enjoy reading."

"On this page, I see the boy, but I don't see the bike. Other children are riding bikes, but this boy isn't, and he looks sad and left out. On this page, there is some kind of a party. I see a cake with candles. I think it must be a birthday party. On this page, the boy is outside, and he has the bike. I bet he got the bike for his birthday! Now, I see him riding the bike. He is riding with the other kids and looks very happy. I think I would like this book because it is a happy book. The boy gets a bike. I like bikes and birthdays, too, so this would be a fun book to read."

"Now that I know I would like to read it, I am going to look at the words in the first few pages of the book and decide if it is 'easy,' 'just right,' or 'too hard for now.' First, I am going to go back to the cover and see if I can read the title. The title of this book is *The New Bike.* Now, I am going to try out the first two pages. I will read the words and put down a finger for any word I can't figure out. This sentence says, '*All the children on*—I don't know that word, and I can't figure it out, so I will put my thumb down and keep reading—*street had bikes. They rode their bikes to school. They rode their bikes around the*—I don't know that word, so I will put my second finger down. *Josh wanted a bike. Josh wanted to ride with his friends'.* I have read these two pages and have only missed two words. A book would be easy if I could read almost every word, and it would be too hard for now if I had all five fingers of my hand down after reading the first two pages. This is a 'just right' book for me. There were two words I didn't know, but I know what is happening in the story, and

I might figure out those words later if I keep reading. I don't have to be able to read every word to enjoy a book, but I shouldn't miss more than four words on two pages."

The teacher continues to demonstrate with two more books how students can decide if they will like a book and if it is "easy," "just right," or "too hard for now." For the second book, she doesn't miss any words on the first two pages and decides it is an easy book, but she will read it anyway because it is about a girl and her cat. For the third book, she misses five words on the first two pages. With all the fingers of one hand down, she decided that this book is too hard for right now, and it will be better to wait until later in the year to try to read this book on her own. Since this is a book she really likes, she suggests that "maybe I can ask the teacher to read it during the teacher read-aloud."

After demonstrating these procedures for determining if a book is easy, just right, or too hard for now, the teacher lets the children try these methods out on some books. Children pick up books and look at the pictures to determine if the book will be interesting to them. Then, they see if they can read the title and use the "five finger" rule on two facing pages. An easy book is a book with no more than one word they can't figure out on these two pages. A just right book has two to four words. If all five fingers of one hand are down, indicating five hard words on the two pages, then that book is probably too hard for now. Children are told that they might enjoy looking at the pictures of a too-hard book—particularly if it is an informational book with lots of pictures—but they also need to spend some of their reading time with a "just right" book.

When children are reading chapter books, the procedure has to change a little because there are few pictures to help you decide. Most of us who read the latest fiction best-sellers make our decisions about which books we like by reading the "teaser" on the back cover and perhaps reading the first page or two. Often, we know we will like a book because we have read other books by this author or because we like just about every book of this genre.

Older children who might not appreciate the Goldilocks analogy often can relate to a riding a bike analogy. Riding along on level ground with few problems is like reading a "just right" book. Sometimes you are riding uphill, however, and this is a bit more of a challenge. Other times, you are riding downhill—fast and free—just relaxing and enjoying the ride. Hard books are then labeled "uphill" books, and easy books are labeled "downhill" books. Teachers who use these terms report that older children like them and use them to describe the books when they conference with the teacher. "This was an uphill book for me, but it was about baseball, so I kept reading because I love baseball!" After much practice with these book-choosing procedures, some teachers post a chart to remind children of the steps for choosing a book.

How to Choose a "Just Right!" Book:

1. Look at the cover and the pictures to see if you think you will enjoy reading this book.

2. If you enjoyed other books by this author, or if this is your favorite type of book or a topic you are particularly interested in, then you will probably enjoy this book.

3. Read the first two pages, putting down a finger for each word you can't figure out.

    0-1 unknown words = easy book ("downhill book")

    2-4 unknown words = just right book

    5 unknown words = too hard for now ("uphill book")

4. Spend most of your Self-Selected Reading time with "just right" books.

5. It is okay to spend some time reading "easy" ("downhill") books you really like and "too hard for now" ("uphill") books you are really interested in.

These procedures are not perfect, and should not be taught to kindergartners or early first-graders. When children are reading books with very few words on a page, missing four words is too many. But, from the middle of first grade on, the five-finger rule works most of the time to help children understand the concept of what a "just right" book is and lets them become independent in selecting books they can read.

Why Not Just Assign Children to a Text Level?

One of the questions commonly asked when discussing the issue of helping children learn to select text they will enjoy and can read is, "Why not just determine the level of text children can read and have them read only from that level?" Knowing the levels for some of the texts in your classroom and knowing the reading levels of your children is an important consideration for any balanced reading program. In Four-Blocks classrooms, teachers do use oral reading records and comprehension measures to determine reading levels for children. When choosing texts for Guided Reading, teachers consider the level of the text in deciding how much and what kinds of support children will need in order to read that text.

Self-Selected Reading is the time each day when your children's reading interests and their intrinsic motivation to read should be paramount in your mind. You want children to decide what kinds of books they like and to learn to determine which books they will be able to read so that they will be able to do this on their own—in the public library or in a bookstore where there are no numbers to tell them what they can and cannot read. Limiting students to a particular level of text would be inconsistent with the spirit and goals of the Self-Selected Reading Block. During your weekly conferences with children during Self-Selected Reading, however, be sure to monitor that most of what they are reading is "just right" for them. Knowing the reading levels of your children and the levels of some of the texts in your room will help you to entice children toward text they can read. In the next chapter, learn how conferences can become "conversations rather than interrogations," as well as some tricks for nudging children toward "just right" text without limiting or labeling them. By teaching children how to choose text they can read, you are promoting independent reading. When students learn how to choose books they can read, they will be able to do this on their own at the library or in the bookstore.

Just for Kindergarten and Early First Grade—Three Ways to Read a Book

Imagine for a moment a four- or five-year-old child who is lucky enough to live in a home where a bedtime reading ritual is carried out nightly. This lucky child has a bookshelf behind his bed containing about 40 books which he owns, and in a separate spot, three books which he has checked out on one of his weekly trips to the public library. Dad, Mom, or the baby-sitter—whoever is in charge that night—reads to him for about 15 minutes. First, one of the new library books is read. Next, the child chooses an old favorite, *Are You My Mother?* by P. D. Eastman, and it is read (probably for the 100th time!).

The child then makes his nightly plea to "look at my books for a few minutes," and the caretaker leaves with a promise to come back in 10 minutes and give him a final hug and turn out the light. When the child is alone, he picks up *Are You My Mother?* and his teddy bear and proceeds to "read" this book to his bear. If you could be a "fly on the wall" and listen in on his reading, you would notice that he has the whole story straight and all the refrains are repeated verbatim.

But, he makes up the rest of the story, getting the general gist of the text, but not reading the exact words. What this preschool child is doing is something called "pretend reading," and it is a stage almost every child goes through.

Children want to do what adults do! They watch adults drive, and they pretend to drive. They watch adults cook, and they pretend to cook. If they watch adults read, they pretend to read and the books they can pretend with are the ones they know well from having those books read over and over to them.

If you return to the young child's room from the example just before the caretaker comes back to turn the light off, you will see this soon-to-be-reader telling his stuffed bear about his favorite trucks from his informational book on trucks.

"This is a garbage truck. The garbage truck comes to our house early on Thursdays."

"This is a dump truck. I have a dump truck out in the sand pile."

"This is a big rig. I am going to be a truck driver when I grow up—and a fireman!"

Four- and five-year-olds who have books and someone to read these books to them regularly show two consistent early reading behaviors—they "pretend read" familiar stories, and they "read and talk about the pictures" in favorite informational books, often books about trucks and other vehicles.

Not all children who arrive at our kindergartens and first grades have been this lucky. For many children, their experience with books and being read to has been minimal or nonexistent. If anyone read to them, it was probably in a large "preschool" group, and books were read once or twice at most. There was no opportunity for these children to hear favorite stories read again and again, or to return regularly to ponder the pictures in a favorite informational book. Young children move into print by approximating the behaviors of real readers.

In kindergarten and early first grade, your young children need to learn that there are three ways children their age read books.

> "There are some books you can read by reading the words. As you become a better reader, you will be able to read more and more of the books in our room by reading the words. Another way children your age read books is by pretending you are reading the book. You do this by telling the story of a familiar book. Finally, you can read a book by talking about the pictures in it, whether it's about trucks or dinosaurs or zoo animals."

At the beginning of the year in your teacher read-aloud, demonstrate these three ways to read. The first several times you read books, such as *Are You My Mother?*, *Rainbow Fish*, or *Hattie and the Fox,* read them the normal way—by reading the words. Once the children know the story well, however, demonstrate how they could pretend to read one of these books, even though there are lots of words they don't know yet, simply by telling the story and using the pictures as prompts.

> "Let me show you how my son David used to read *Are You My Mother?* to his teddy bear. David had just started school and didn't know many words yet, but he knew the story well, so he would pretend to read it to his bear."

The teacher would then "pretend read" the story, saying the refrains exactly, but filling in the other parts as they made sense. If the same procedure is repeated with *Rainbow Fish* and *Hattie and the Fox,* children will soon catch on to how you can "read books before you can read!"

Once the children understand how to pretend read by telling a familiar story, the teacher demonstrates how to read and talk about the pictures in simple informational books. After reading a book about trucks several times, the teacher would show them how, "David read the truck book to his Teddy bear." This procedure would be repeated with some other (mostly picture) informational books. The talk here should be more than just naming the pictures. Young children don't just go through and name the pictures, "garbage truck; dump truck; big rig." Rather, they talk about them and share the connections they make to their own lives, "I play with my dump truck." or "My uncle used to drive a big truck like that."

By the time you are a month into the school year, all your kindergartners and early first-graders will know that there are three ways to read, and they will have watched you demonstrate these three ways. They know that they can read books by reading the words if they know most of the words, they can tell the story of a familiar book, or they can talk about the pictures. Once students know this, the individual reading part of the Self-Selected Reading Block can get off to a successful start. No one says, "But I can't read yet!" The students read books in the way that "lucky" children with books and bedtime reading rituals at home read books. During this early part of the year, as the children read, go around the room and notice how they are reading a book and support and join them in whatever way they are using. If a child is "pretend reading a story," pretend read a few pages with that child. If a child is talking about the pictures in an informational book, talk about the pictures with that child. As the year goes on and children learn more words and strategies for figuring out words, then the books they were pretending to read and talking about the pictures in become books they can "really read!"

By the time this happens, all the children will be used to the daily time when they settle down by themselves with a book they have chosen to quietly read to themselves—or a stuffed animal—in whatever way they can.

A caution needs to be added to the discussion here. You would not do this with children older than kindergarten or first grade (unless developmentally or in their knowledge of English, they were at the "five-year-old" stage). Children in second grade and above who pretend to read stories or just look at pictures day in and day out during Self-Selected Reading are not going to make the growth they need to make from spending most of their time reading "just right" books. "Three ways to read books" is a kindergarten-and-first-grade-only strategy. Children at that age love to pretend read stories and talk about pictures, but they also love being able to "really read" and will move to that kind of reading as soon as they possibly can.

Convincing Older Struggling Readers to Read

The children who read the least in our schools are preteen children who don't read well and don't like to read. Having a Self-Selected Reading Block is important for all children, but if the children you teach don't read at grade level and have given up on books, it is critical. There are many things that help one become a better reader. Learning more sight words and strategies for identifying words helps students read better and that is the focus of the Working with Words Block. Learning comprehension strategies and applying them differentially to story and informational text also helps students read better, and that is the focus of the Guided Reading Block. Writing is an approach to reading, and children who write regularly become better readers. Both self-selected writing and focused writing are included in the Writing Block. But, as important as these all are, the amount of reading is more important. Students who read only what is assigned—and often only the part of the assigned reading that someone is actually making sure they read—will never achieve the proficient reading levels required in today's society.

Now, if you teach older reluctant readers, this isn't telling you anything you don't see on a daily basis in your classroom. You know that your students need to get the "reading habit," and you know they don't have it. You also know that having a daily Self-Selected Reading Block in which you read to the students and then they read books of their own choosing would help—if you could get them to do it!

Here are some of the ideas that teachers of older struggling readers use to make Self-Selected Reading work for them:

Use several short "grabbers" from a newspaper for your teacher read-aloud.
Bring in your local daily paper or the *USA Today*. Divide it into sections. Read a short piece or part of a piece from several different sections. Don't forget the cartoons—editorial and others. Read an ad—if it is for something your kids are all interested in. Try to create an "I was reading my paper this morning, and I just had to share this with you" atmosphere. Keep your reading quick. If the article is long, read a little and summarize the rest—or read a little and claim you haven't had time to finish it, but will finish it tonight, letting the students wonder how it came out. If possible, get friends or other teachers to give you their copies of the newspaper and divide these into sections. Make these copies available for any student who wants to read them on his own. Newspaper reading is one of the most common adult-reading habits, and struggling readers who develop the newspaper reading habit will improve their reading ability.

Occasionally, read parts of a favorite magazine for your teacher read-aloud.
Communicate to the students that magazine reading is part of your regular routine. If you subscribe to a weekly or monthly magazine, bring it in after you have read it and communicate to students that there is something in here "you just had to share." As with newspapers, keep the pace fast and leave the students wanting to know more. You can get magazines from the library and share parts of them with your students. Sometimes, libraries or bookstores will give you magazines that are past their date. If there are objectionable things in other parts of the magazine, cut out only the section you want to share with your students. Punch holes in interesting magazine articles and put them in a binder so that students can read them if they choose. As the number of articles grows, separate them into different binders—sports, animals, music groups, cool cars, etc. Magazine reading is another common adult reading habit which struggling readers often find more satisfying and available than book reading.

Include some easy series books, chapter books, and informational books in your teacher read-aloud.
In Chapter 3, you learned about the wide range of materials available for Self-Selected Reading—on all different levels. Hopefully, if you teach older reluctant readers, you are finding ways to get some of these materials in the hands of your students. But, many children won't read these books if they consider them to be in the least bit "babyish" or "uncool." When you read a book to your students and show your obvious pleasure in the book, you have "blessed" it, and it will now be acceptable reading. The books you will get the most payoff from reading aloud to your students are those from a series or written by the same author. Read two of the *Magic Tree House* or *Junie B. Jones* books, and then magically produce the others. (Hide these away until you have read a couple

of books from the series aloud, and the students' mouths are watering!) Read a couple of the animal books written by Gail Gibbons, and then entice them with the others. Read the biographies of Tiger Woods and Michael Jordan, and then show student examples of other sports biographies. Then, when you read the second book of a series or type or author, they should be expecting that there are "more where these came from," and you won't want to disappoint them.

Increase the individual reading time of your Self-Selected Reading block very gradually.
This is important for all students, but it is particularly important if most of your students don't like to read. Start with five, six, or seven minutes. Use a timer and stop when time is up even if the students protest. Do not add a minute until they all settle down and read something—newspapers, magazines, books—without hassling you or each other. When you get to 10 minutes, stay there until the students ask for more time. Then, agree to add time, but let the class know that they can't take out too much time just to read when there is so much work to do! Soon, the students will be viewing their personal reading time as something valuable and will try to talk you into more!

Enforce the "No Wandering" rule, but make sure students have lots of choices of interesting material wherever they are reading.
Older children especially like to make choices and "have some say" in where they read. Determine places in the room where students can read and decide how many people can be at each spot. Use a deck of index cards with the students' names written on them to decide who gets to pick their spot first. Shuffle the cards and dismiss the students from the teacher read-aloud to go to whatever spot they choose (if it is still available when their cards come up). If students violate the "No Wandering" rule or the "Reading Quietly" rule, send them to a special table and then join them at that table, making clear your disappointment.

Don't even think about formal conferences until the reading habit is firmly established.
Conferencing is important, and as soon as the daily reading time is firmly in place, you should begin holding individual conferences with your students. But, if you "abandon" your students too soon, you may never achieve the quiet, peaceful atmosphere that will allow you to do good conferences later in the year. When you first begin the individual reading time, circulate quietly around the room. Drop down and join your students at eye level. "Ooh and aah" about what they are reading—in a very quiet voice.

> "Ooh, you're reading the article about my favorite basketball team. I read everything about them and love to go to their games."

> "Aah, that looks like a great book! I love books with lots of photos of real people. I haven't read that one yet, but I think I might read parts of it to everyone tomorrow."

> "Ooh, you are reading my favorite magazine. I subscribe to that one and just let everything else go and sit right down and read it when it comes in the mail."

Move from student to student quickly, and resist the urge to ask anyone to read to you or ask a comprehension question. (Leave your clipboard on your desk!) Remember the goals of this block. You want your students to become intrinsically motivated to read, to develop their reading interests, and to read things on their own reading level. By "oohing and aahing" in a whisper voice (which, by the way, makes the other students wonder what secrets you and the lucky recipient are sharing), you are giving your reluctant readers positive feedback about their reading—a rare occurrence for most of them.

Adopt a class of kindergartners as your reading buddies.
There is one legitimate way that you can get your students to read all the wonderful books they can now read and enjoy, but wouldn't be caught dead with. Arrange for a class of kindergartners (or first-graders) to visit with you on a weekly basis. Tell your student that the kindergarten teacher needs their help. (Everyone wants to be needed!) Explain about all the things kindergartners need to learn about books—how to hold books, where to begin reading, how to follow the print, how books tell stories and have lots of information, etc. Then, explain that although the kindergarten teacher reads to the whole class, it is not the same as reading to one child. The kindergarten children in the group cannot all see the pictures and can't ask questions and make comments that help them understand and develop a love of books. Tell the class that, after a lot of thought, the kindergarten teacher and you decided that the kindergartners need to be read to one-on-one, and they can help by becoming big reading buddies to initiate the kindergartners into a love of books and reading!

Once your students are hooked on their important roles, produce a box of books the kindergarten teacher has suggested for reading to the children. Make sure you include lots of old favorites that will be familiar to your students. Almost all struggling readers have had Dr. Seuss books, *Clifford* books, and familiar tales like *The Gingerbread Man* and *The Three Little Pigs* read to them. They usually remember these books fondly and are actually eager to read them—if you legitimize this for them. Let them share their memories of these books with you. Then, read a few of the books to your students. Be sure they understand that you are reading the books to them so that you can teach them how to read to little children. Choose one child to be the "pretend kindergartner," and model with that child as the others watch. Demonstrate how to talk together about the pictures and encourage the younger child to make comments and ask questions. When you have read the first book, ask for another volunteer to pretend to be the kindergartner and read a second book. Continue reading these books to them—two or three a day for several days—and then let each student choose a book to read to his kindergarten buddy. Tell the students that they need to practice reading the book at least twice to be sure they can read it aloud with excitement and good expression. Circulate as they read and encourage them. Don't worry if they don't read every word exactly right. The kindergartners won't notice (hopefully!), and your students are getting some critical practice reading easy text which will improve their fluency and their confidence.

Once the weekly "reading buddy" visits are up and running, you won't need to spend as much time preparing. The same set of 30-40 books can be used for the entire year and just rotated from child to child. You may want to post a list of who has been read which book. Then, each week your students can choose a book they haven't read yet to their kindergarten buddy. Some of your students may take the initiative of finding books from the school library for their buddies to enjoy. Encourage this, but make sure the librarian knows that they are checking out these "easy" books to read to their kindergarten buddies.

Buddy reading programs have been very successful in improving the confidence and attitude of the big buddies toward reading, and the little buddies look forward to and benefit from the one-on-one weekly reading time. This is a "win-win" activity for all involved, and easy to do with the resources and people right there in your school!

7

READING CONFERENCES

Imagine yourself sitting at the pool or on a beach, reading a book that you are really enjoying. A friend comes over and joins you. The two of you catch up on "life," and then your friend notices the book.

> "Oh, I see you are reading the latest Jan Karon book. I've read the first two and am about to begin the third one. I heard that in your book, the main characters don't live in Mitford any more. Are her books as good without all the Mitford characters?"

You then launch into a glowing recommendation for the new book set at the coast. Perhaps you read aloud a part you really like and the two of you get into a great conversation about Jan Karon, which leads to other books you both like and ends with a promise from your friend to loan you the latest book by Maeve Binchy—an author you have never read, but who your friend believes is equal to Jan Karon in her ability to create memorable characters. Though you are skeptical about anyone being able to match Jan Karon in character creation, you can't wait to read it and see.

In the real world, this is how we talk about books. We have conversations about them with people who have read them and with people who haven't. We share what we like and sometimes even read aloud a memorable part. We get ideas for other books to read—and sometimes, someone even gives us or loans us a book they think we might like. These informal conversations about books with friends and relatives play a big role in motivating our reading and sparking our reading interests. As much as possible, try to conduct your conferences with children as conversations centered on their book.

Getting Started with Conferences—Modeling and Practicing

Once your Self-Selected Reading Block is up and running smoothly and the children are in the habit of reading quietly for at least 12 minutes, you can begin to hold regularly scheduled conferences with all your students. (Prior to this, you have been circulating around the room, sharing books with children in hushed voices, and reminding children of what is appropriate during Self-Selected Reading time.) As with everything you want the students to learn how to do, model and demonstrate what the conference will look like several times before you begin.

Here is what a teacher might say to explain and demonstrate to the children what will be expected of them in the conference:

"Boys and girls, you are doing a spectacular job of reading quietly and making good choices each day during Self-Selected Reading. I love sharing your books with you and learning about what you like to read as I come around and have a quick chat with you. I wish we had more time to talk about each of your books, so starting next week, I am going to schedule everyone for a one-to-one conference with me every week. We won't have much time to talk, so you will have to be prepared to share with me the best parts of your book and make the best use of the time we have. Let me show you how you can prepare for your conference and what we will do in the conference."

"The first thing you have to do is to decide what book you want us to talk about. You might have read lots of books since our last conference, but we will only have time to talk about one, so you have to choose. I'm going to ask Joey to come up here and help me by pretending he is getting ready for his conference." (The teacher has chosen Joey to be first because he is a "with it," verbal kid and will catch on quickly to what is expected, and he won't be shy about talking about what is on his mind.)

"Joey, find three or four of the books you have read recently during Self-Selected Reading, and bring them up here." (Joey finds some books and comes and sits next to the teacher.)

"Now, Joey, take a minute and look through these books, and choose one that you would most like to talk with me about." (Joey looks at the books and chooses a book about a dog.)

"Good, now look through that book and find a page or two that you want to read to me. Pick the most interesting or the funniest part that you know I will want to hear." (Joey looks through the book and comes to a favorite page and smiles up at the teacher.)

"Good, now read that page aloud to practice one time. You want to read it as well as possible, so that I will enjoy it as much as you do." (Joey reads the page aloud. He stumbles on one word but the teacher tells him to just continue and they will talk about that word during the conference. The teacher then hands Joey an index card, and asks him to write the name of the book and the number of the page he read aloud on the index card. If it is a picture book with no page numbers, he will have to count the pages to determine the page number. He then uses the index card to mark that page.)

"Good job, Joey! Now for the thinking part. You chose this book and this page. I want you to think aloud about how you would explain to me why you chose this book and this page. What did you really like about this book?" (Joey talks about the book. The teacher encourages him to turn to other pages in the book to show pictures that explain what he is talking about.)

The teacher then turns his attention back to the rest of the class, which has been watching intently. He says, "Joey is ready for his conference with me. He has chosen one book he really likes. He has chosen a page or two from that book to read to me and practiced reading. He has his index card bookmark in the right place with the book title and page number written on it, and he has thought about what he wants to tell me about his book."

"Now, we are going to pretend again, but this time we will pretend Joey is coming for his conference. I am going to sit at the back table where we can have a private place to talk. You will, of course, be quietly reading in your places while Joey and I are having our conference, but for today, I will let you listen in so you know what will happen. Let's all move to the back table." (Everyone moves to the back table. The teacher directs the children to stand around the table where they can watch and listen.)

"I will sit here (facing the classroom), and Joey will sit here (facing away from the classroom). This is Joey's conference sheet." (The teacher holds up conference sheet and shows that it has a place for the date, the title and author of the book, and the number of the page read. There is also a place to indicate if this book seems to be "easy," "just right," or "hard," as well as a place for the teacher to comment about Joey's reaction to the book or what he plans to read next.)

READING CONFERENCE SHEET		CHILD'S NAME Joey			
DATE	TITLE	AUTHOR	PAGE	LEVEL	COMMENTS/FUTURE PLANS
11/26	Harry the Dirty Dog	Gene Zion	4	JR	excellent retelling
12/3	Frog and Toad Together	Arnold Lobel	10	JR	first chapter book
12/10	Polar Bears	Gail Gibbons	6-7 (no page #s)	Hard	chosen for interest

With all the students watching, the teacher holds a conference with Joey. The teacher greets Joey promptly and writes the date, title, and author on his conference sheet. Joey turns quickly to the page(s) he chose to read and reads them aloud. He reads the difficult word correctly now and explains how he "got it." Joey and his teacher decide that this was a "just right" book for him because there were a few words on some pages he had to figure out. The teacher indicates the page number Joey read aloud on his conference sheet and codes it "JR" (just right) under the "Level" column. Joey shares some of his favorite parts of the book with the teacher. The teacher "oohs" and "aahs" about the book, saying "Ooh, this is a funny book. The dog is very mischievous, but very cute. Aah, what a great illustration. I can see why you chose this book." The teacher writes "Loves animal stories" in the Comment section on his sheet, and the conference ends.

For the next several days, the teacher chooses one child each day to role play choosing a book and preparing for the conference in front of the class. Then, the class moves to the back table and listens as the teacher and students actually have the conference. After watching several of these "mock conferences," the children are ready and eager for their own conference with the teacher. The teacher posts a schedule to show who will conference on which day, along with this chart of reminders.

Getting Ready for Your Reading Conference

1. Pick the book or other reading material you want to share.

2. Pick a part to read aloud to me and practice reading this.

3. Write the title and page number on a bookmark and put it in the right place.

4. Think about what you want to share with me:

    What you like about this book

    Why you chose these pages to read

    Other good parts of the book

    Your plans for our next conference

Doing the Conferences

Try to conference with every child once a week. If you have 22 children, you would have four or five children scheduled each day. (If you have more than 25 children, you probably need to go to an every sixth-day schedule because it is nearly impossible to do more than five good conferences on a single day.) Depending on how long the class's reading time is, each conference would last 3-5 minutes. Three to five minutes is not very long, but if the children are prepared for their conferences, you can get quite a bit accomplished in that short period of time. In Four-Blocks classrooms, no activity gets a very long time period on a daily basis, but critical components are repeated day-in and day-out, week-in and week-out. If you started your conferences after the first month of school, persevered until the end of the year, and had a four-minute (on average) conference with each child for 32 weeks, you would have had over two hours (4 minutes times 32 weeks = 128 minutes!) of one-to-one, intense interaction with each of your students about their reading. When children are prepared and conferences are held consistently, the minutes add up! Four-Blocks teachers will tell you that they know much more about each individual reader than they did when teaching in more traditional ways. A lot of what teachers know about each child is learned through the weekly conference.

When scheduling the children for conferences, consider which children need more time and attention. Many teachers spread out their most struggling readers across the conference days, then conference with that day's struggling reader first and give that child a few extra minutes. Struggling readers often have the most difficulty choosing books they can read and will enjoy. Many teachers keep a "stash" of enticing, easy books at the conference table. After sharing the book the reader has brought with him, the teacher asks the child if he would like some help picking some good books that are "just right" to read for the next week. If the child "bites," the teacher and the child try out some of the books in the special basket. They talk about some of the pictures to help the child decide if this is a book he would like to read. Then, the child reads the first two pages, and using the "five-finger" rule, the teacher and the child jointly decide if the book is "easy," "just right," or "too hard for now." The books the child chooses are "checked out" to him and available, along with whatever books are available to everyone else, until next week's conference.

The children at the other end of the reading scale—your advanced readers—often also need special attention during their reading conferences. Teachers often spread their advanced readers across the days and give them an extra minute, especially if the books they are choosing are very easy for them. Imagine a child who is a very good reader and loves mysteries. This child is reading "lickety-split" through all the "grade level" mysteries she can find. After the child has shared her reading with the teacher, the teacher might reach into a special stash of books and pull out two mysteries checked out from the school or public library. Together, the teacher and child preview the books, talking about the chapter titles and considering if the child thinks this would be a really good mystery. Next, the teacher encourages the child to read the first two pages. The child might encounter a few hard words, and the teacher will need to explain that this book is harder than the ones the child has been reading.

"This mystery is harder than second-grade level, but it looks really interesting, and it might be 'just right' for you. I checked it out from the library because I know how much you love mysteries, and I thought you might really like this one. It is harder than the mysteries you have read so far, and you will probably have to work at some of the words. But if you think you want to try it, I will check it out to you. Be sure and let me know next week what you thought of it."

Few readers, children or adults, can resist the lure of a book of the type they like to read that someone has found just for them!

After conferencing with one of your struggling readers and one of our advanced readers, conference with two or three of your more "average" children. Conferences with these children are quicker because they generally come prepared for the conference and have less difficulty selecting books they like at the "just right" level. It worries some teachers that the "average readers" aren't getting quite as much attention in the weekly conferences as the struggling and advanced readers. But, you must remember that being fair means giving everyone what they need—not necessarily giving everyone the same amount of everything. Having children spend some quality time reading materials at the "just right" level is important to the reading growth of all students. Although teachers try to stretch the Self-Selected Reading Block to provide instructional level materials for all children, the struggling and advanced readers are the ones who are most apt to be reading materials that are too hard or too easy during this block.

Making Self-Selected Reading Conferences Work for You

Teachers often express concerns about Self-Selected Reading. They worry that they are not "doing the conferences right," or that they haven't "gotten around to conferences yet." The conference is an extremely important part of the Self-Selected Reading Block. Remember the goals of the Self-Selected Reading Block:

- To introduce children to all types of literature through the teacher read-aloud.
- To encourage children's reading interests.
- To provide instructional-level reading.
- To build intrinsic motivation for reading.

Reading aloud to the children and providing them with time, choice, and materials to read will go a long way toward meeting these goals. But, in the individual conferences, you encourage each child's reading interests as you "ooh and aah" over each child's choices and the progress that child is making. You can determine if the books they are choosing are too hard or too easy and "nudge" them toward appropriate books. Intrinsic motivation for reading—the desire to do it because it is enjoyable—is greatly enhanced as the children anticipate their weekly visits with you about their books.

To help teachers with the problems they have experienced and their basic feelings of discomfort about the concept of individual reading conferences, some ideas and suggestions are listed below. Consider your own comfort level as you decide how to make reading conferences work for you:

Limit the time for individual reading, and increase the time gradually as the children show you they can sit quietly and read.

Use the "dismissal to their own books" routine described in this chapter, and have your children observe how others get to their places quickly and begin reading quietly. Don't hesitate to call a child back who does not follow the procedures. After a serious conversation with him, accompany the child to his spot and help him get started reading quietly. Use a timer to time the reading and one-minute increases. Make it a sign of your children's maturity and responsibility that they can "read quietly for nine minutes after only doing this for two weeks!"

Don't start conferences until the routines for reading are well-established and your children are following these routines.

The time you invest during the first weeks of school, making sure that everyone knows where they will read, how they will read, and how to choose "just right" books they will enjoy, will pay off for you as the school year continues. Before you begin individual conferences, rotate quietly throughout the room, stopping for no more than a minute with individual children and discussing their books with them in a very hushed voice.

Make sure your children know how to get ready for their conferences.

Remember that it is the child's job to prepare for the conference. Your job is to "ooh" and "aah" and help children who need help in selecting "just right" books. Many teachers express concern about the conferences because they "don't know what questions to ask" and are not sure how much instruction or what kind of instruction to give. In Four-Blocks classrooms, two of the blocks—Guided Reading and Working with Words—are referred to as the "bossy" blocks. During this half of the literacy time, teachers are very bossy. Teachers tell the children exactly what to do, and then assess that they have done it. The other two blocks—Writing and Self-Selected Reading—are much more "teacher behind the child" blocks. The child prepares for the conference, and you follow the lead of the child. If a child comes to the conference unprepared, ask that child to go and get prepared and try to fit the child in after you have conferenced with the other children scheduled for that day. Most children like this "one-on-one" time with their teacher and try hard to impress the teacher by coming prepared. If you will do the modeling and practice described earlier in the chapter, most children will come prepared and eager to talk with you about their reading.

Don't waste time waiting for children to come to their conferences.
The time for conferences is always very short. If you are conferencing with five children and the rest of the class is reading for 18 minutes, you have about three minutes to devote to each child. (Remember that you don't have to divide the time exactly equally. You might give four to five minutes to a struggling and/or an advanced reader and less time to your average readers.) Regardless of how much time you have and how many children you need to conference with, you don't have minutes to spare as each child is called and "ambles" over to the conference table. You certainly don't have time to discover that one of your conferees has decided this is a good time for a bathroom break! Many teachers gather up the children they will conference with that day at the end of teacher read-aloud and take these children with them to the conference area. The children get the materials they want to conference on and sit nearby, practicing for the conference or reading something else, while they wait their turn.

Keep your records simple and consistent with the goals of Self-Selected Reading.
The Self-Selected Reading conference is not a time for the teacher to be so busy writing things down that there is no time to encourage and respond. Remember, you want this weekly one-on-one time to be a conversation, not an interrogation. You want each child to look forward to his or her time with you and to anticipate your positive responses to their reading interests. This is not a time for taking formal running records, although you do make a judgment about the "just right" level of the book after listening to the child read and talk about the book.

Make new rules as you see the need for them.
Anyone who has not taught your children could never anticipate all the problems that might occur. Next year's class of children might "think up some new tricks" this year's class never dreamed of. For example, in one class, a few children kept bringing back the same book to conference on, week after week. This had not occurred the year before so the teacher, not having anticipated this, had not made it part of the conference procedures. When it became a problem, however, she added a new step for preparing for the conference:

> *Bring a book you haven't shared with me before—unless you are halfway through a long book and want to bring it back ONE time and tell me how it turned out.*

That solved the problem! When a new problem occurs, think about what will solve the problem, be consistent with the goals, and make a rule!

When kindergartners and first-graders are reading in the "three ways," conference with them in whichever way they are reading.

Remember that you've taught your kindergartners and early first-graders that they can read by reading the words, telling the story, or talking about the pictures. When children are in the "three ways," stage, you will need to alter your conference procedures to reflect that. When a child brings a book to conference, you should ask how the child is reading the book. If the child responds that he or she is telling the story, encourage that child to turn to some favorite pages and tell the story that goes with those pages. If the child responds that he or she is talking about the pictures, talk with the child about and enjoy the chosen favorite pictures. Note the appropriate reading method on the conference record sheet. As the teacher, you get to enjoy all three ways that children are reading, but as the first-grade year goes on, more and more children will bring books in which they can read the words. You should encourage them to do so. If certain children persist in bringing books in which they tell the story or talk about the pictures, a new rule may need to be made.

You can bring a book to tell the story or talk about the pictures, but you must also bring a book in which you are reading the words.

Consider conferencing by moving to the child instead of having the child move to you.

Most teachers like to have a quiet place where they can conference with children. Some teachers, however, feel that the conference works better if they move to the children. Early in the year, before you begin formal conferences with children, you are moving around and stopping to speak with individual children. Some teachers like to continue having their conversations in the "child's space." If you want to move to the child's space to confer, be sure that the children know when they will be conferenced with so they can prepare for the conference. Conversations are more likely if you and the child can talk "face to face," so you may want to carry a small chair with you so that you can sit and talk with the child at eye level.

Don't let one child ruin things for everyone else.

In many classrooms, there is a child who finds it extremely difficult to sit away from the teacher and do what is required. If you have such a child, consider having the child do his or her reading in a spot within arm's reach of where you will conference. Make sure the child has lots of choices of reading material available, and "compliment" the child with occasional looks and gestures to show him or her that you are noticing his or her good, quiet reading behavior. Some teachers "check in" with this child for just a few seconds before each conference. If the child expresses the desire to read where the others are reading, discuss the rules and what will be required and give him a chance to show that he can do it. But, if the child demonstrates that he needs to be in close physical proximity to you in order to have a peaceful, quiet classroom atmosphere, keep that child close to you. Different children have different needs, and different classrooms of children have different "chemistries." Try to allow everyone as much choice and freedom as you can, but enforce the rules and procedures needed so that the children can concentrate on their reading and you can enjoy your conferences.

View your reading conferences as conversations—not interrogations!

Assessing and monitoring comprehension is an important part of any balanced reading program. In the Guided Reading Block, you monitor and assess comprehension and progress toward your curriculum goals. But in Self-Selected Reading, the focus is different. Remember the goals of this block. You want children to become intrinsically motivated to read, to find their own reading interests, and to read books on their "just right" level. You want children to look forward each week to their "one-on-one" special time with you. No one looks forward to being questioned and interrogated! We all like to talk to people who care about the things we care about, including what we are reading and what we think about our reading. You and the children will find the conferences something to look forward to if you both view them as "talking about books with a friend."

Consider the possibility that you might not feel comfortable conferencing because you have never had anyone conference with you!

Teachers tend to teach the way they were taught. When there is something that we would like to do, but we just "can't imagine it," it is usually because it was never done with us, and we have never seen another teacher do it. If you never had a teacher who sat down each week and had a one-on-one conversation with you about your reading, don't you wish you had? Having weekly conversations with children about their reading is not difficult, and in fact, is usually viewed by teachers and children as one of the most pleasant times in the day. If you would like to conference, but you haven't quite gotten around to it, it might just be because you have never experienced a conference like this or seen it done. Take a leap of faith. Use the procedures described here—or others you know your children need—and "jump in!" Thousands of teachers just like you do it every day and love it. You can, too!

8

SHARING, RECORD KEEPING, AND ASSESSMENT

So, you have your Self-Selected Reading Block up and running relatively smoothly. You are reading to your kids from a variety of different materials. Your children are reading quietly (most days!), and you are holding individual conferences (a.k.a. CONVERSATIONS!) with your children on a weekly basis. Here are just a few more things to think about. How will you promote the collaboration amongst your students about their reading that we know motivates children to read? What kind of records should be kept? How can you assess the effectiveness of your Self-Selected Reading Block?

Sharing

Do you ever talk about books with your friends? Do you swap books? When you finish a particularly poignant book, do you think about who would enjoy it? The three authors of this book—Pat, Dottie, and Linda—are longtime book swappers. Dottie and Pat are often on airplanes together and inevitably, after catching up with each other, books are pulled out and a little book talking goes on before they settle down to read. It is fairly common for Pat to return home reading the book Dottie was reading on the trip out, and of course, Dottie is reading the book Pat has finished. If a particularly interesting book does not get finished during the trip, Pat or Dottie often part company with luggage in hand and a promise that, "I will save this book for you and give it to you next week." Linda, who lives in another state, does not see Pat or Dottie as often, but when they are together, at some point the conversation turns to the books they've read, and they often save books for each other.

Sharing ideas and talking with others about books is an important factor in developing engaged and motivated readers. Self-Selected Reading is the backdrop for providing children with many opportunities to talk about books and other ideas that are of great interest to them. Children frequently comment that they have chosen a book because someone told them about it. The more books children know about, the more books they are likely to read. In Four-Blocks® classrooms, regular opportunities for children to share books with one another are provided. In some classrooms, the sharing is done daily. In other classrooms, some time is set aside each week (or every other week) for children to share books. While sharing is an important motivator, it must be remembered that the major activities in Self-Selected Reading are the teacher read-aloud, the individual reading by the children, and weekly conferences with the teacher. Teachers have to be careful not to let the sharing time take away from these other important activities. In general, if children share daily, you should limit this sharing time to five to eight minutes. Weekly or every-other-week sharing sessions would last for 20–30 minutes.

Here are some ways you might organize your sharing sessions:

Partner Quickshares

In Partner Quickshares, children are paired with a partner, and each child has one minute to tell something interesting, exciting, or important about what they read today during Self-Selected Reading. The partners change each day so that children get to interact with many different classmates over a few weeks time and see all the different types of books their peers are reading and are excited about. In order to do this efficiently and get the children together, some procedures are needed. The following example illustrates the system one clever teacher devised for Partner Quickshares.

At the end of Self-Selected Reading time each day, the children look up at the teacher as she takes out her index cards and shuffles them. The index cards have the names of all the children in the class written on them. The teacher then calls out the names on the first two cards. Those two students will be sharing partners for today. Then, the next two cards are called, and those two become sharing partners, and so on. Cards are called until all the children are partnered up. (The last group may be a threesome if an odd number of children are present on this particular day.) As the names are called, the second child called in each partnership moves SILENTLY to where the first child is seated and waits there until all the partners are in place. Once all the partners are in place, the teacher sets a timer for one minute. The second child (who moved to the first child's spot) shares first. After one minute, the teacher signals the children to switch turns and the other child has one minute to share.

Partner Quickshares usually happens at the end of Self-Selected Reading each day and can be easily done in five minutes once the routines are established. If you are going to use Partner Quickshares on a daily basis, it is important to remind children as they begin reading that they will be sharing with someone—and that they will have only one minute. They should be on the lookout for something "INTERESTING, EXCITING, or IMPORTANT" as they read. The use of these three words is important because they apply equally well to story or informational text. You may want to write these three words on the board in big letters as a reminder to children as they are reading. Some teachers who do Partner Quickshares give each child a sticky note to mark the interesting, exciting, or important part of the text so that it can quickly be found for sharing. This is a little extra motivation because children love having that sticky note! As the partners are sharing, circulate around the room, and listen in. When the two minutes are up, pick one or two of the tidbits shared and share these with the whole class, telling them that, "This was just too good to miss!"

Other teachers set aside a half-hour sharing/selecting time once a week. Children share their favorite books and parts of books for the week during the first 15 minutes, and then select books for the next week during the last 15 minutes.

Four Share

In Four Share, four children share together and specific roles are assigned. The first person in each group shares by reading or telling about one or two pages in his or her book. The second person then says one thing he or she liked about what was shared. The third person asks one question. The last person tells something he or she would like to know more about. When this first round of sharing is complete, the second person in the group shares and all the roles shift one position. The third person tells one thing he or she liked. The fourth person asks one question. The first person who shared now has the role of thinking of something he or she would like to know more about.

Four Share is an excellent way to share books, but as with Partner Quickshare, some routines must be established so that the groups are formed quickly and the children understand their roles. Here is how one teacher handles the routines. He calls on the children to form the groups by shuffling index cards with the names of the children written on them. Before calling each foursome, he designates each group by where they will meet. The first four children always go to the science corner, the second four always go to the back table, the third four always go to the computer area, the fourth four always go to the reading rug, the fifth four always go to the blackboard area, and the last four always go to the teacher's desk (the most popular spot, to be sure!) As they go to their areas, the teacher has them count off "1-2-3-4" in the order their names were called and sit in a circle in this order. When all the groups are in place—two minutes maximum once the routines are established— the first person called (#1) is the first sharer, the person to the right is #2 whose role is to "say something you liked," and the next person to the right of #2 is #3 who has the "ask a question" role. The last person is #4, and this child assumes the "tell something you would like to know more about" role. With the children sitting in a circle and knowing where to begin, it is easy then for the next person (#2) to become the sharer and continue around the circle.

Four Share takes about 20 minutes and thus would be a weekly or every-other-week activity, rather than a daily one. On the day that you are going to do Four Share, you will need to schedule some extra time or do a very quick teacher read-aloud—perhaps something from a newspaper or magazine that will intrigue the children but won't take very long to read. Children need to know that they will be doing Four Share that day before they begin their reading, so that they will be prepared. Some teachers give everyone one index card to mark the page or pages they will share. Be sure the children know that they can read or tell about the pages. Some children (particularly in that preteen stage) are very shy about reading to their peers, and everyone should have the option of talking and perhaps showing pictures. Four Share is a wonderful way to make sure your students are doing the kind of higher-level thinking about books that adult readers do. Children who are in the habit of thinking of something they like, a good question, and something they want to know more about as they listen to someone else's book, will soon begin to do this kind of critical thinking with their own books. No small accomplishment!

Finally, Four Share is a good way to share because children like it. They like the fact that you never know which group you will be in or which place in the room your group will meet. They like the fact that there is predictability in what they will do in the group. They also like having their turn at doing "all the roles."

Tea Parties

Well, actually, juice and popcorn are more common for this than tea and crumpets—but it's the same idea! In many classrooms, a weekly or every-other-week "tea party" is held. Books are shared, and food is served. In some classrooms, children or room mothers sign up to bring the food. In other classrooms, the school (and often the teacher) provides the food and drink.

Depending on how comfortable your children are with talking about books, you may want to leave the discussions open and free flowing, making sure that everyone who chooses to has a chance to share; or you may want to use the "Four Share" or some other structured method of determining the order and content of the sharing. Regardless of how the sharing is arranged, you will probably want to use the shuffled cards to determine the groups. Letting the children choose who they want to share with almost always creates a group of "outsiders." When you as the teacher choose, kids tend to fuss if you don't put them with their best friends. The cards are arbitrary and children do understand the need to go with "the luck of the draw!" Besides, the groups change every time so they might get to share with their best friends next time!

Whole Class Share

Letting a few children share something from their books each day is the most common way sharing happens in classrooms, and in most cases, is the least effective. If this is the way you have been doing your sharing, ask yourself how effective it is in helping you meet the goals of Self-Selected Reading. Do your children look forward to this time each day? Do they pay attention to the person who is sharing without having to be reminded to "give Billy your attention"? Do most of your children look forward to their day to share, and do they share interesting parts of what they are reading? Do you see other children eager to read the books that have just been shared?

In many classrooms, whole-class sharing is being done in a very "it's on the schedule, we have to do it" way. Children who don't know what to say mumble a few inaudible words. Other children who are being called on for comments and questions say things like, "I liked your book" and "Why did you choose this book?" It is a rare classroom in which the whole-class sharing time seems to be giving you the money's worth for the time and energy invested in it. But, this rare classroom does exist, and here are some of the things that are common across these classrooms.

Teachers who do successful whole-class sharing limit the number of children who share to one or two per day. These children know well ahead of time which day they will share, and they are reminded by the teacher that this is their day to share so they might want to use some of their Self-Selected Reading time getting ready to share. Early in the year, the teacher often arranges for the one or two children who will share to be included in the group of children he or she will conference with that day. During their conference, the teacher helps this child decide what would be an interesting or exciting part to share and whether to read that part or tell about it.

The sharing itself happens every day, but is limited to five minutes. The child has one minute to read or tell about the chosen part—and they can do it in a minute if they have rehearsed and had prompting as needed by the teacher! Then, the teacher models something specific he or she liked:

"I liked this part because I knew what was going to happen, but Ramona didn't. I love to be able to figure out what is going to happen, and then have it really happen!"

"I love this page because of the pictures. They are real photographs of sea turtle babies, and they make me wish I could be there to really see them."

"I love Dr. Seuss books, too, and this is one of my favorite pages because it is just such fun to say all the silly words. I love the pictures, too."

Next, the teacher invites a child or two to tell what they particularly liked about the book. If the child's response is "I liked your book," the teacher prompts the child to be more specific.

After telling something specific he or she liked and then letting a child or two tell something specific, the teacher models an "I wonder" statement.

"I wonder if Ramona is going to be able to keep the dog. Does anyone know how this book ended?"

"I wonder where the closest place is to here that there are sea turtles. I would love to be able to go somewhere and really see some."

"I wonder how Dr. Seuss got his ideas for books. No one has ever been able to write funnier books."

The teacher then turns to the children and asks what this book makes them wonder about. Very few children will say, "I wonder why you chose this book!"

So, based on these observations, if you want to do "whole class shares" as your book sharing activity, limit the number of shares to one or two each day, keep it short, rehearse and help the sharers prepare, and model specific "I like" and "I wonder" statements. If you do this, your sharing time will motivate your children to read a variety of books, raise the level of their thinking, and keep everyone from sitting there with "Will this ever end?" looks on their faces!

When teachers do sharing with the whole class, they often use some "prop" to designate that it is the sharing portion of the Self-Selected Reading Block. A reader's chair (DeLinda DeLightfull called it a share chair!), a microphone, and a cardboard television set are some props used by teachers to spice up the whole class share. One teacher uses a large cardboard box painted to look like a television set to get the idea across to her class that the sharing or "selling" of a book should be done quickly. (Some children take longer to tell about the book than to read the book.) Telling about a book, or what you like about the book, in a few sentences is a skill that many children need to learn! The teacher might reinforce this by saying, "We love to share our favorite books, but when it is our turn to use the TV set we need to do a quick commercial for our book. Everyone has one minute on TV to sell or tell the class about a favorite book they have read recently." One-by-one, four or five children come up each day and go behind the suspended TV and sell or tell the class about their book. After a minute, the timer goes off and the next student is ready to sell and tell about his or her book.

Record Keeping

When thinking about record keeping, there are two questions to consider. What kind of records should the teacher keep? What kind of records should children keep?

The Teacher's Records for Self-Selected Reading

What kind of records you keep, how you keep them, and what you keep them in have a lot to do with your teaching style. Some teachers are "neat and tidy." They like to have everything in straight rows and columns, and keep their records in alphabetical order in some "neat and tidy" notebooks or binders. (Bet their drawers at home are neat and tidy, too!) Other teachers keep different kinds of records. They jot down notes on whatever is handy, and eventually they sort these out and put them someplace where they (hopefully) can find them when they need them. Many very good teachers have records of what their students do but could never be described as "neat and tidy."

This point is made primarily to encourage you "not-so-neat-and-tidy types" to go ahead and keep your records in whatever form suits your personality, and not to give up on record keeping because your records don't look like those of your "neat and tidy" teacher friend. What matters is not how the records are kept, but that some kind of records are made of children's behaviors during Self-Selected Reading, and particularly records of their responses and book choices during your weekly conferences. Your record system should be simple and done in a form that suits you, and, most importantly, the records you keep should relate directly to the goals of Self-Selected Reading.

One of the goals for Self-Selected Reading is to expose children to the widest possible variety of literature during the teacher read-aloud. Our strong belief about kids and books is that a child who doesn't like to read is just a child who hasn't found the right book—YET! Do you remember the first truly wonderful book you read as a child—a book you just couldn't put down? (Pat actually remembers reading her first (of many) Bobbsey Twin books and finishing it under the covers by flashlight!) As you learned in the previous chapters of this book, the teacher read-aloud has a powerful effect on promoting children's motivation and interests. You may want to list all the books you read aloud to your children, and then tally them under the type of book they are. This record will let you demonstrate that you have indeed read to your students "from all the different sections of the bookstore."

Another goal for Self-Selected Reading is that much of the reading children do should be at the right level for them. This is important for all children, but is most important for your struggling and your advanced readers. The conferencing chapter described how to nudge children towards books on their level (while, at the same time, remembering that reading something easy that you are interested in is a good reading behavior that all good readers engage in). One of the things you would want to make a record of is the level of the book the child brought to the conference with you. Specifically, you want to know if the book seems "easy (downhill)," " just right," or "hard (uphill). As described in Chapter 7, you make this determination by listening to the child read and talk about a page or two.

The final two goals of Self-Selected Reading are that the child become intrinsically motivated to read, and that each child develop personal reading interests. You can make judgments about children's intrinsic motivation to read by observing their behaviors during the individual reading time and by their responses and enthusiasm during the conference. At the beginning of the year, not all children settle in happily with their reading material, and some children just bring "whatever" to the conference because the weekly conference is just one more thing they have to do! Note their reluctance and lack of enthusiasm as a comment on your weekly conference record. Many teachers are shocked to look back at their early-in-the-year conference records and realize how unmotivated many of their children were! The increase in motivation and accompanying enthusiasm happens gradually. Weekly judgments about enthusiasm recorded in some fashion will let you document each student's progress toward your intrinsic motivation goal.

The development of reading interests can be determined by keeping a list of the books each child brings to the weekly conference. As the year goes on, you should be able to look at the list of books you have conferenced with each child on and know who is becoming a mystery reader, who likes animal books, and who likes books about sports and sports figures. Of course, children, like adults, will branch out occasionally and read a book outside their usual interests if everyone is reading and talking about a book, but most readers read books from one or two genres or on a couple of "high-interest-to-them" topics.

Remember the earlier caution against requiring children to read from a variety of genres during Self-Selected Reading? In Four-Blocks classrooms, there are two places in which variety of genres is emphasized. Teachers expose children to the widest range of genres during the teacher read-aloud, and they require that everyone to read from a wide range of genres during the Guided Reading Block. In Four-Blocks classrooms, everyone will know how mysteries (biographies, informational books about animals, plays, etc.) are written and will have listened to the teacher read at least one of each aloud and will have read at least one of each during the Guided Reading Block. It is important that all children leave elementary school knowing how to comprehend all the different genres they will be required to read. But, adult readers have specific reading interests and spend most of their time reading in their area of interest, children whose reading interests are being developed will show this clearly as they bring the same type of book to the conference almost every week. A list of books you conference with each child about will let you know how each child is moving toward the goal of developing his or her personal reading interests.

Your records should be simple, in a style suitable to you, and they should relate to the goals of the block. Here is one child's weekly conference sheet. Notice that individual conferences began in October. The teacher has held nine conferences with Joey.

READING CONFERENCE SHEET		CHILD'S NAME Joey			
DATE	TITLE	AUTHOR	PAGE	LEVEL	COMMENTS/FUTURE PLANS
10/4	Encyclopedia Brown #16	Donald J. Sobol	24	JR	Likes mysteries; good choice.
10/11	Encyclopedia Brown #16	Donald J. Sobol	50	JR	Likes the solution at the end of the book.
10/18	Football Jokes & Riddles	Matt Christopher	no page #s	Easy	Showed me the list of referee signals and demonstrated them.
10/25	The Home Run Mystery	Gertrude Chandler Warner	37	JR	Reads with fluency. Discussed mystery so far.
11/6	The Home Run Mystery	Gertrude Chandler Warner	121	JR	Predicts ending.
11/13	Eagles of America	Dorothy Hinshaw Patent	14	JR	Fascinated by eagle facts; good comprehension
11/20	Dr. Martin Luther King, Jr.	David Adler	24-25	Easy	Easy biography; remembers details.
11/27	Indian in the Cupboard	Lynne Reid Banks	23	Hard	Challenge book.
12/4	Indian in the Cupboard	Lynne Reid Banks	75	Hard	Good retelling of the story so far.

Children's Records

In many classrooms, children keep lists of books they have read, often called reading logs. While this is a fairly pervasive practice, it is unclear if it is a productive one. You may see some young children who spend more time finding their reading log and assiduously copying the name and author of the book in their log than they did reading the book! You may also watch some older children flip through the pages of a book—speed reading it at a pace even Evelyn Woods wouldn't believe—and then logging it in as a "read book."

"But I need to know which books my children have read," you may be thinking. This is agreed, but the reading log is not necessarily a true indicator of what they have read. Some children forget to log in books, or just can't find that log when they need it ("I know it's in this desk somewhere!") Other children, who like to have the longest list, pick books just because they are short and easy and they can list lots of them. Reading logs also discourage rereading of favorite books—an activity lucky children with their own little libraries at home engage in all the time.

Although it is a widespread practice, requiring children to keep logs of the books read during Self-Selected Reading is more trouble than it is worth. It takes time away from reading, and may actually work against the goals of having children reading books at their level, becoming intrinsically motivated to read, and developing their own personal reading interests. The better indicator of what children have read is the record the teacher keeps as a result of the weekly conferences. Every child conferences once each week with the teacher, and a record will be made of one book per child. No child will have a list any longer than any other child. Rereading of favorite books is allowed during Self-Selected Reading (although children are required to bring a book they haven't conferenced on before to the conference unless they were halfway through a long book last time and want to bring it back and tell you how it came out).

If your school requires your students to keep reading logs, keep the logs very simple—author, title, and date only. It is further suggested that there be no "count" of the books listed and that the logs be kept private, with no child looking at another child's log. Allow books to be logged in only after the Self-Selected Reading time is up so that time will not be taken away from reading. Finally, do not worry about the logs too much. Children who fabricate or stretch the truth a little might be less inclined to do this when no one is paying attention to how long their lists are. Children who can't find their log or who forget to log some books (perhaps because they got so "into" their reading, or because they are just not neat and tidy kids!) will not get fussed at, and thus will avoid setting up some negative attitudes towards books because they don't do their logs well.

There is one kind of reading list children should keep—and it is a list that many adult readers have—a list of books they want to read! Now, here's a list that is in keeping with the goals of Self-Selected Reading! Periodically, perhaps after some book sharing, children should be encouraged to add to their list of "Wanna Read" books. The teacher might model this by posting a list of books the children want her to read aloud and adding to that list whenever a book occurs to someone.

"Look, it says on the back of this book that the author has written another book about.... I am going to add that to the list of Future Read-Aloud books and be on the lookout for it."

"Miss Wheeler told me about a great book she is reading to her class. I am going to put it on our Future Read-Aloud books list so I don't forget about it."

The other kind of list some teachers keep is a list of students who want to read a book that the teacher has read aloud to the class. One third-grade teacher has popsicle sticks on which she has written each child's initials. When the teacher finishes reading aloud a book to the class, she asks everyone who wants to be on the list to read the book to put their stick in a box. She closes her eyes and picks sticks from the box. A student records the initials in the order called out and posts the list in a special place on the board. The first child called gets the book immediately. When that child finishes, he consults the list and hands it to the next person, and so on.

Tortillas
by
Margarita Gonzalez-Jensen
HR ✔
TP ✔
JB _____
KG _____
CL _____
JS _____
AG _____
EP _____

SHARING, RECORD KEEPING, AND ASSESSMENT

Assessment

If you have done everything suggested in the record-keeping section of this chapter, you have done most of what you need to do to assess progress toward the goals of Self-Selected Reading. Your record of books read aloud, categorized by types, demonstrates your progress toward making sure that your students know about all the different kinds of books there are. Your conference records demonstrate how much reading children are doing at the "just right" level. The list of books read and your comments about the students' reading allow you to make judgments about their intrinsic motivation for reading and the development of their own reading interests. This just goes to prove that observation and good record keeping—neat and tidy or not—is the most valid and reliable way of assessing critical goals in a literacy program.

There is just one more piece of evidence you might like to collect. Some teachers construct a simple form which asks children about their favorite books, authors, and topics (a reproducible form is on page 107). They administer this form early in the school year, halfway through the school year, and again at the end of the school year. You and your children will be amazed at the growth in reading interests and motivation they gain across the year by comparing their answers to these three simple questions. Early in the year, their answers are often vague. Everyone lists Beverly Cleary or Marc Brown as their favorite author, and *Charlotte's Web* gets lots of choices for best book. As the year goes on, the students' responses demonstrate their growing book sophistication. Try it and see if you, too, are not amazed by the students' growth. It will help sustain you in doing your daily Self-Selected Reading Block when time and test pressures threaten to undermine your determination.

Name _____   Date _____

What Do You Like to Read?

1. List the two best books you have read in the last few months and tell why.
   Best Book _____
   Why?

   Next Best Book _____
   Why?

2. List your two favorite authors and tell why.
   Favorite Author_____
   Why?

   Next Favorite Author _____
   Why?

3. List the two types of books you like best. Be as specific as you can.
   Favorite Type of book_____
   Why?

   Second Favorite _____
   Why?

There is a clear relationship between how much children read and how well they read. Children who read a lot read better than children who only read when they have to! Many schools feel that they don't have time in their busy day to have teachers read aloud to children and let the children read whatever they choose. "We have to take the tests. Our children have to do well or they get retained, and we get put on probation," teachers and administrators lament. All classrooms need a time each day for teachers to read to children so that children develop "the reading habit." Schools with lots of struggling readers feel the pressure of tests and accountability the most and are least apt to provide daily Self Selected Reading time. These are the very schools that need it most. Children who read more read better. Children who read better score better on tests. Children who have "fallen in love" with their own special books and authors read even when they are not being watched. The benefits of a daily Self-Selected Reading time are hard to see on a day-to-day basis, but they add up over time. Good readers read lots of books; struggling readers read very little. To be a good reader, you must read a lot. To have students that read a lot is the "mega-goal" of Self-Selected Reading!

CHILDREN'S BOOKS CITED

The Adventures of Captain Underpants by Dav Pilkey (Scholastic, 1997).

Alexander and the Horrible, Terrible, No Good, Very Bad Day by Judith Viorst (Antheneum, 1976).

An Alphabet Book of Cats and Dogs by Sheila Moxley (Little, Brown & Co., 2001).

Animalia by Graeme Base (Harry N. Abrams, 1993).

Are You My Mother? by P. D. Eastman (Random House, 1988).

Arthur Makes the Team by Marc Brown (Little, Brown & Co., 1996).

Aunt Isabel Tells a Good One by Kate Duke (E. P. Dutton, 1992).

Back Home by Gloria Jean Pinkney (Penguin Putnam Books, 1999).

Basketball ABC: The NBA Alphabet by Florence Cassen Mayers (Harry N. Abrams, 1996).

Because of Winn-Dixie by Kate DiCamillo (Candlewick Press, 2000).

Biscuit by Alyssa Satin Capucilli (HarperCollins, 1999).

Brown Bear, Brown Bear, What Do You See? By Bill Martin, Jr. (Holt, Rinehart & Winston, 1970).

The Brand New Kid by Katie Couric (Doubleday, 2000).

The Bridge to Teribithia by Katherine Patterson (Thomas Y. Crowell, 1977).

By the Sea: An Alphabet Book by Ann Blades (Kids Can Press, Toronto, 1985).

Charlotte's Web by E. B. White (Harper Trophy, 1999).

Chato's Kitchen by Gary Soto (Paper Star, 1997).

The Chocolate Touch by Patrick Skene Caitling (William Morrow & Co., 1979).

Chicken Socks by Brod Bogert (Boyds Mills Press, 2000).

Clifford books by Norman Bridwell (Scholastic).

The Creepy Thing by Fernando Krahn (Houghton Mifflin Co., 1982).

Dear Mr. Henshaw by Beverly Cleary (Dell, 1983).

Dinosaur Detectives by Peter Crisp (Dorling Kindersley Publishing, 2001).

Dogsong by Gary Paulsen (Aladdin Paperbacks, 1999).

The Doll House Murders by Betty Ren Wright (Holiday House, 1983).

Dr. Martin Luther King, Jr. by David A. Adler (Holiday House, 2001)

The Dumb Bunnies by Sue Denim (Scholastic, 1994).

Eagles of America by Dorothy Hinshaw Patent (Holiday House, 2001).

Eating Fractions by Bruce McMillan (Scholastic Trade, 1991).

Encyclopedia Brown and the Case of the Mysterious Handprints by Donald J. Sobol (Bantam Skylark, 1986).

Encyclopedia Brown: Boy Detective by Donald J. Sobol (Econo-Clad Books, 1999).

Eruption! The Story of Volcanoes by Anita Ganeri (Dorling Kindersley Publishing, 2001).

Faithful Elephants by Yukio Tsuchiya (Houghton Mifflin Co., 1988).

A Family Is Special by Darwin Walton, (Steck-Vaughn Company, 2002).

Fast Sam, Cool Clyde, and Stuff by Walter Dean Myers (Viking Press, 1988).

Favorite Greek Myths by Mary Pope Osborne (Scholastic, 1991).

Finding Providence: The Story of Roger Williams by Avi (Harper Trophy, 1997).

Fly Away Home by Eve Bunting (Clarion Books, 1993).

Football Jokes and Riddles: 50+ Facts and Funnies to Keep You Laughing by Matt Christopher (Little, Brown & Co., 1997)

The Fourth Little Pig by Teresa Noel Celsi (Steck-Vaughn Company, 1993).

Frog and Toad Together by Arnold Lobel (Harper Trophy, 1979).

Frog on His Own by Mercer Meyer (E. P. Dutton, 1993).

The Gift Giver by Joyce Hansen (Houghton Mifflin Co., 1991).

Gingerbread Baby by Jan Brett (Putnam, 1999).

The Giving Tree by Shel Siverstein (HarperCollins Children's Books, 1987).

Grandpa, Grandpa by Joy Cowley (Wright Group, 1988).

Guess Who's Coming, Jesse Bear by Nancy White Carlstrom (Simon & Schuster, 1998).

Harry the Dog titles by Gene Zion (HarperCollins).

Hattie and the Fox by Mem Fox (Simon & Schuster, 1988).

The Home Run Mystery (Boxcar Children #14) by Gertrude Chandler Warner et al (Albert Whitman & Co., 2000).

A House for Hermit Crab by Eric Carle (Simon & Schuster, 1988).

In the Tall, Tall Grass by Denise Fleming (Henry Holt & Co., Inc., 1991).

Indian in the Cupboard by Lynne Reid Banks (Doubleday, 1982).

Insects by Robin Bernard (National Geographic Society, 2000).

Love You Forever by Robert Munsch (Firefly Books, 1989).

Junie B. Jones Is a Party Animal by Barbara Park (Random Library, 1997).

The Little Prince by Antoine Saint-Exupery (Harvest Books, 2000).

The Lion, the Witch, and the Wardrobe by C. S. Lewis (HarperCollins, 1994).

The Magic School Bus: At the Water Works by Joanna Cole (Scholastic, 1990).

The Magic School Bus: Lost in the Solar System by Joanna Cole (Scholastic, 1990).

Lions at Lunchtime (Magic Tree House 11) by Mary Pope Osborne (Random House, 1998).

Maniac McGee by Jerry Spinelli (Little, Brown & Co., 1990).

Martha Speaks by Susan Meddaugh (Houghton Mifflin Co., 1995).

Miss Nelson Is Missing by Harry Allard (Houghton Mifflin Co., 1977).

Miles of Smiles: Kids Pick the Funniest Poems by Bruce Lansky (Meadowbrook Press, 1998).

Mr. Popper's Penguins by Richard and Florence Atwater (Little, Brown & Co., 1992).

Mufaro's Beautiful Daughter by John Steptoe (William Morrow & Co., 1987).

My Great Aunt Arizona by Gloria Houston (HarperCollins, 1992).

My Puppy Is Born by Joanna Cole (Mulberry Books, 1991).

The New Kid on the Block by Jack Prelutsky (William Morrow & Co., 1984).

NBA Action from A to Z by James Preller (Scholastic, 1997).

No More Homework! No More Tests!: Kids' Favorite Funny School Poems by Bruce Lansky (Meadowbrook Press, 1997).

Oh, How I Wish I Could Read by John Giles (JGC/United Publishing Corps, 1995).

Paddington Bear by Michael Bond (HarperCollins, 1998).

Paddington's ABC by Michael Bond (Puffin Books, 1996).

The Plains of Africa by Morgan le Fey (A fictional book in *Lions at Lunchtime (Magic Tree House 11)* by Mary Pope Osborne).

Polar Bears by Gail Gibbons (Holiday House, 2001).

Rainbow Fish by Marcus Pfister (North South Books, 1996).

Rain Makes Applesauce by Julian Scheer (Holiday House, 1985).

The Relatives Came by Cynthia Rylant (Alladin Books, 1985).

Rosa Parks: My Story by Rosa Parks (Dial Books for Young Readers, 1992).

Ruby the Copycat by Peggy Rathmann (Scholastic, 1997).

Sarah, Plain and Tall by Patricia MacLachlan (Harper & Row, 1985).

See You Later, Gladiator by Jon Scieszka (Viking Children's Books, 2000).

Sheila Rae, the Brave by Kevin Henkes (Mulberry Books, 1996).

Shrewbetinna's Birthday by John Goodall (Atheneum, 1971).

Something for Nothing by Phoebe Gillman (Scholastic, 1993).

Swimmy by Leo Leonni (Alfred Knopf, 1991).

Tell Me A Story, Mama by Angela Johnson (Orchard Books, 1992).

Tool Box by Gail Gibbons (Holiday House, 1988).

Tortillas by Margarita Gonzalez-Jensen (Scholastic, 1994). Available from Scholastic School Books division.

Trumpet of the Swan by E.B. White (HarperCollins Children's Books, 2000).

The Velveteen Rabbit by Margery Williams (Alfred A. Knopf, 1990).

The Very Hungry Caterpillar by Eric Carle (Putnam Publishing Group, 1984).

The Wall by Eve Bunting (Houghton Mifflin Co., 1992).

What's It Like to Be a Fish? by Wendy Pfeffer (HarperCollins, 1996).

Winnie-the-Pooh by A.A. Milne (Puffin, 1992).

Yellow Bird and Me by Joyce Hansen (Clarion Books, 1991).

Zoe's Web by Thomas West (Scholastic, 2000).

Zoo Animals by Mary E. Pearson (Steck-Vaughn, 2002).

At the time of publication, children's books cited were in print or available at libraries or bookstores.

REFERENCES

Alexander, P.A., Kulikowich, J.M., & Hetton, T.L. (1994). "The Role of Subject Matter Knowledge and Interest in the Processing of Linear and Nonlinear Texts." *Review of Educational Research, 64*, 210-253.

Allington, R.I. (1983). "The Reading Instruction Provided Readers of Differing Reading Abilities." *The Elementary School Journal, 83*, 548-559.

Allington, R.I. (1984). "Policy Constraints and Effective Compensatory Reading Instruction: A Review." Paper presented at the annual meeting of the International Reading Association, Atlanta, GA. (ERIC Document Reproduction Services No. ED 248456).

Allington, R.I. (1986). "Policy Constraints and Effective Compensatory Reading Instruction: A Review." In J. Hoffman (Ed.) *Effective Teaching of Reading: Research and Practice* (pp. 261-289). Newark, DE: International Reading Association.

Allington, R.I. (1991). "The Legacy of 'Slow It Down and Make It More Concrete.'" In J. Zutell & S. McCormick (Eds.), *Learner Factors/Teacher Factors: Issues in Literacy Research and Instruction* (pp. 19-30). Chicago: National Reading Conference.

Almasi, J. (1995). "The Nature of Fourth-Graders Sociocognitive Conflicts in Peer-Led and Teacher-Led Discussions of Literature." *Reading Research Quarterly, 30*, 314-351.

Anderson, R. C., & Pearson, P.D. (1984). "A Schema-Theoretic View of Reading." In P. D. Pearson, M. Kamil, P. Mosenthal, & R. Barr (Eds.) *Handbook of Reading Research.* New York: Longman.

Anderson, R. C., Wilson, P. T., & Fielding, L. G. (1988). "Growth in Reading and How Children Spend Their Time Outside of School." *Reading Research Quarterly, 23*, 285-303.

Artley, S. A. (1975). "Good Teachers of Reading—Who Are They?" *The Reading Teacher*, 26-31.

Barrentine, S. J. (1996). "Engaging with Reading through Interactive Read Alouds." *The Reading Teacher, 50*, 36-43.

Brennan, T. P., & Glover, J. A. (1980). "An Examination of the Effect of Extrinsic Reinforces on Intrinsically Motivated Behavior: Experimental and Theoretical." *Social Behavior and Personality*, 8, 27-32.

Calkins, Lucy (1994). *The Art of Teaching Writing*. Portsmouth, NH: Heinemann.

Cameron, J., & Pierce, W. D. (1994). "Reinforcement, Reward, and Intrinsic Motivation: A Meta-Analysis." *Review of Educational Research, 64*, 363-423.

Campbell, J. R., Hombo, C. M., & Mazzeo, J. (2000). "NAEP 1999 Trends in Academic Progress: Three Decades of Student Performance." *Education Statistics Quarterly, 2*, 31-36.

Coley, J. D. (1981). "Non-Stop Reading for Teenagers: What We Have Learned and Where We Go From Here." Paper presented at the annual meeting of the College Reading Association, Louisville, KY. (ERIC Document Reproduction Service No. ED 211951).

Cunningham, A. E., & Stanovich, K. E. (1998). "What Reading Does for the Mind." *American Educator*, Spring/Summer, 8-15.

Cunningham, P. M. & Allington, R. L. (1998). *Classrooms That Work, 2nd ed.* New York: Addison, Wesley Longman.

Cunningham, P. M. & Hall, D. P. (1996). *Building Blocks: A Framework for Reading and Writing in Kindergartens That Work.* (Video) Clemmons, NC: Windward Productions.

Cunningham, P. M. & Hall, D. P. (1997). *Month-by-Month Phonics for First Grade.* Greensboro, NC: Carson-Dellosa.

Cunningham, P. M. & Hall, D. P. (1997). *Month-by-Month Phonics for Upper Grades.* Greensboro, NC: Carson-Dellosa.

Cunningham, P. M. & Hall, D. P. (1998). *Month-by-Month Phonics for Third Grade.* Greensboro, NC: Carson-Dellosa.

Cunningham, P. M. & Hall, D. P. (1999). *The Four Blocks: A Framework for Reading and Writing in Classrooms That Work.* (Video) Clemmons, NC: Windward Productions.

Cunningham, P. M., Hall, D. P. & Sigmon, C. M. (1999). *The Teacher's Guide to the Four-Blocks®.* Greensboro, NC: Carson-Dellosa.

Cunningham, P. M. & Hall, D. P. (2000). *True Stories from Four-Blocks® Classsrooms.* Greensboro, NC: Carson-Dellosa.

Cunningham, P. M., Hall, D. P. & Cunningham, J. W. (2000). *Guided Reading the Four-Blocks® Way.* Greensboro, NC: Carson-Dellosa.

Cunningham, P. M., Hall, D. P. & Defee, M. (1991). "Nonability Grouped, Multilevel Instruction: A Year in a First-Grade Classroom." *The Reading Teacher, 44*, 566-571.

Cunningham, P. M., Hall, D. P. & Defee, M. (1998). "Nonability Grouped, Multilevel Instruction: Eight Years Later." *The Reading Teacher, 51.*

Cunningham, P. M., Moore, S. A., Cunningham, J. W. & Moore, D. W. (2000). *Teachers in Action.* New York: Addison, Wesley Longman.

Deci, E. L. (1975). *Intrinsic motivation.* New York: Plenum Press.

Deci, E. L., Valerand, R. M., Pelletier, L., & Ryan, R. (1991). "Motivation and Education: The Self-Determination Perspective." *Educational Psychologist, 26*, 325-347.

Duke, N. (2000). "3.6 Minutes Per Day: The Scarcity of Informational Texts in First-Grade." *Reading Research Quarterly, 35*, 202-224.

Elley, W. (1989). "Vocabulary Acquisition from Listening to Stories." *Reading Research Quarterly, 24*, 174-187.

Elley, W. B. (1992). "How in the World Do Students Read? IEA Study of Reading Literacy." International Association for the Evaluation of Educational Achievement. (ERIC Document Reproduction Services No. ED 360613).

Fawson, P. C., & Fawson, C. (1994, May). "Conditional Philanthropy: A Study of Corporate Sponsorship of Reading Incentive Programs." Paper presented at the meeting of the International Reading Association, Toronto, Canada.

Fountas, I. & Pinnell, G. S. (1996). *Guided Reading*. Portsmouth, NH: Heinemann.

Fountas, I. & Pinnell, G. S. (2001). *Guiding Readers and Writers Grades 3-6*. Portsmouth, NH: Heinemann.

Fountas, I. & Pinnell, G. S. (1999). *Matching Books to Readers*. Portsmouth, NH: Heinemann.

Gambrell, L. B. (1996). "Creating Classroom Cultures That Foster Motivation." *The Reading Teacher, 50*, 14-25.

Gambrell, L. B. (1981). "Sustained Silent Reading—A Time for Teachers." *The Reading Teacher, 34*, 836-38.

Gambrell, L. B. & Jawitz, P. (1993). "Mental Imagery, Text Illustrations and Young Children's Reading Comprehension." *Reading Research Quarterly*, 28, 264-276.

Gambrell, L. B. & Marinak, B. (1997). "Incentives and Intrinsic Motivation to Read." In J. Guthrie and A. Wigfield (Eds.), *Reading Engagement: Motivating Readers through Integrated Instruction* (pp. 205-217). Newark, DE: International Reading Association.

Gambrell, L. B., Wilson, R. M., & Gantt, W. (1981). "Classroom Observations of Task Attending Behaviors of Good and Poor Readers." *Journal of Educational Research*, 74, 400-404.

Garves, D. H. (1995). *A Fresh Look at Writing*. Portsmouth, NH: Heinemann.

Guthrie, J. T., Schafer, W., Wang, Y. Y., Afflerbach, P. (1995). "Relationships of Instruction to Amount of Reading: An Exploration of Social, Cognitive, and Instructional Connections." *Reading Research Quarterly, 30*, 8-25.

Hall, D. P. & Cunningham, P. M. (1997). *Month-By-Month Reading and Writing for Kindergarten*. Greensboro, NC: Carson-Dellosa.

Hall, D. P. & Cunningham, P. M. (1998). *Month-by-Month Phonics for Second Grade*. Greensboro, NC: Carson-Dellosa.

Hall, D. P. & Williams, E. (2001). *The Teacher's Guide to Building Blocks*. Greensboro, NC: Carson-Dellosa.

Hall, D. P., Prevatte, C. & Cunningham, P. M. (1995). "Eliminating Ability Grouping and Reducing Failure in the Primary Grades." In Allington, R. L. and Walmsley, S. (Eds.) *No Quick Fix*. Teachers College Press, 137-158.

Harris, V. J. (1992). "Multiethnic Children's Literature." In K. D. Wood and A. Moss (Eds.), *Exploring Literature in the Classroom: Content and Methods*. Norwood, MA: Christopher-Gordon, 169-201.

Hayes, D. P., & Ahrens, M. (1988). "Vocabulary Simplification for Children: A Special Case of 'Motherese.'" *Journal of Child Language, 15*, 395-410.

REFERENCES

Hidi, S. (1990). "Interest and Its Contribution as a Mental Resource for Learning." *Review of Educational Research, 60,* 549-571.

Ivey, G. & Broaddus, K. (2001) "Just Plain Reading: A Survey of What Makes Students Want to Read in Middle School Classrooms." *Reading Research Quarterly, 36,* 350-377.

Juel, C. (1988). "Learning to Read and Write: A Longitudinal Study of Fifty-Four Children from First through Fourth Grade." *Journal of Educational Psychology, 80,* 437-444.

Karnoil, R. & Ross, M. (1977). "The Effect of Performance Relevant and Performance Irrelevant Rewards on Children's Intrinsic Motivation." *Child Development, 48,* 482-487.

Lepper, M. R., Greene, D., & Nisbett, R. E. (1973). "Undermining Children's Intrinsic Interest with Extrinsic Rewards." *Journal of Personality and Social Psychology, 28,* 129-137.

Linehart, G., Zigmond, N., & Cooley, W. (1981). "Reading Instruction and Its Effects." *American Educational Research Journal, 18,* 343-361.

Mayes, F. J. (1982). "U.S.S.R. for Poor Readers." *Orbit, 13,* 3-4.

McCombs, B. I. (1989). "Self-Regulated Learning and Academic Achievement: A Phenomenological View." In B. J. Zimmerman & D. H. Schunk (Eds.), *Self-Regulated Learning and Achievement: Theory, Research, and Practice* (pp. 51-82). New York: Springer-Verlag.

McGill-Franzen, A., & Allington, R. L. (1991). "The Gridlock of Low Reading Achievement: Perspectives on Practice and Policy." *Remedial and Special Education, 12,* 20-30.

McLaughlin, D., Bandeira de Mello, V., Cole, S., & Arenson, E. (2000). "Comparison of National Assessment of Educational Progress (NAEP) and Statewide Assessment Results: Report to Maryland on 1996 and 1998 Assessments." American Institutes for Research in the Behavioral Sciences, Palo Alto, CA. (ERIC Document Reproduction Services No. ED 446153).

Mendoza, A. (1985). "Reading to Children: Their Preferences." *The Reading Teacher, 38,* 522-527.

Nagy, W. E., & Anderson, R. C. (1984). "How Many Words Are There in Printed School English?" *Reading Research Quarterly, 19,* 304-330.

Neuman, S. B., & Celano, D. (2001). "Access to Print in Low-Income and Middle-Income Communities." *Reading Research Quarterly, 36,* 8-26.

Oldfather, P. (1993). "What Students Say About Motivating Experiences in a Whole Language Classroom." *The Reading Teacher, 46,* 672-681.

Palmer, B. M., Codling, R. M., & Gambrell, L. B. (1994). "In Their Own Words: What Elementary Children Have to Say about Motivation to Read." *The Reading Teacher, 48,* 176-179.

Paris, S. G., & Oka, E. R. (1986). "Self-Regulated Learning Among Exceptional Children." *Exceptional Children, 53,* 103-108.

Pressley, M., Borkowski, J. G., & Schneider, W. (1987). "Cognitive Strategies: Good Strategy Users Coordinate Metacognition and Knowledge." In R. Vasta & G. Whitehurst (Eds.), *Annals of Child Development, 4,* (pps. 89-129). Greenwich, CT: JAI Press.

Reutzel, D. R., & Hollingsworth, P. M. (1991). "Reading Comprehension Skills: Testing the Distinctiveness Hypothesis." *Reading Research and Instruction, 30,* (2) 32-46.

Routman, Regie (1995). *Transitions, 2nd ed.* Portsmouth, NH:Heinemann.

Smith-Burke, T. M. (1989). "Political and Economic Dimensions of Literacy: Challenges for the 1990's." In S. McCormick & J. Zutell (Eds.), *Cognitive and Social Perspectives for Literacy Research and Instruction* (pp. 1-18). Chicago: National Reading Conference.

Snow, C. E., Barnes, W. S., Chandler, J., Goodman, I., & Hemphill, I. (1991). *Unfulfilled Expectations: Home and School Influences on Literacy.* Cambridge, MA; Harvard University Press.

Stanovich, K. E. (1986). "Matthew Effects in Reading: Some Consequences of Individual Differences in the Acquisition of Literacy." *Reading Research Quarterly, 21*, 360-401.

Stanovich, K. E. (1993). "Does Reading Make You Smarter? Literacy and the Development of Verbal Intelligence." In H. Reese (Ed.), *Advances in Child Development and Behavior*, 24, 133-180. San Diego, CA: Academic Press.

Taylor, B. M., Frye, B. J., & Maruyama, G. M. (1990). "Time Spent Reading and Reading Growth." *American Educational Research Journal, 27*, 351-362.

Turner, J. C. (1995). "The Influence of Classroom Contexts on Young Children's Motivation for Literacy." *Reading Research Quarterly, 30*, 410-441.

Turner, J. C., & Paris, S. G. (1995). How Literacy Tasks Influence Children's Motivation for Literacy." *The Reading Teacher, 48*, 662-675.

Veatch, J. (1959). *Individualizing Your Reading Program.* NY: Putnam.

Wiesendanger, K. D., & Birlem, E. D. (1984). "The Effectiveness of SSR: An Overview of the Research." *Reading Horizons, 24*, 197-201.

Additional References:

4-Blocks Mailrings at *teachers.net* and *www.readinglady.com*

The Four-Blocks Center at *www.wfu.edu/~cunningh/fourblocks*

CALDECOTT MEDAL WINNERS AND HONOR BOOKS
1938–2001

The Caldecott Medal was named in honor of nineteenth-century English illustrator Randolph Caldecott. It is awarded annually by the Association for Library Service to Children, a division of the American Library Association, to the artist of the most distinguished American picture book for children.

2001
Winner:

So You Want to Be President? illustrated by David Small, written by Judith S. George (Philomel Books)

Honor Books:

Casey at the Bat: A Ballad of the Republic Sung in the Year 1888 illustrated by Christopher Bing, written by Ernest Lawrence Thayer (Handprint Books)

Click, Clack, Moo: Cows That Type illustrated by Betsy Lewin, written by Doreen Cronin (Simon & Schuster)

Olivia illustrated and written by Ian Falconer (Simon & Schuster/Atheneum)

2000
Winner:

Joseph Had a Little Overcoat illustrated and written by Simms Taback (Viking)

Honor Books:

Sector 7 illustrated and written by David Wiesner (Clarion Books)

The Ugly Duckling illustrated and adapted by Jerry Pinkney (Morrow)

A Child's Calendar illustrated by Trina Schart Hyman, written by John Updike (Holiday House)

When Sophie Gets Angry—Really, Really Angry... illustrated and written by Molly Garrett Bang (Scholastic)

1999
Winner:

Snowflake Bentley illustrated by Mary Azarian, written by Jacqueline Briggs Martin (Houghton)

Honor Books:

No, David! illustrated and written by David Shannon (Scholastic)

Snow illustrated and written by Uri Shulevitz (Farrar)

Tibet: Through the Red Box illustrated and written by Peter Sís (Frances Foster)

Duke Ellington: The Piano Prince and His Orchestra by Andrea Davis Pinkney, illustrated by Brian Pinkney, written by Andrea Davis Pinkney (Hyperion)

1998

Winner:

Rapunzel illustrated and adapted by Paul O. Zelinsky (Dutton)

Honor Books:

The Gardener illustrated by David Small, written by Sarah Stewart (Farrar)

There Was an Old Lady Who Swallowed a Fly illustrated and adapted by Simms Taback (Viking)

Harlem: A Poem illustrated by Christopher Myers, written by Walter Dean Myers (Scholastic)

1997

Winner:

Golem illustrated and written by David Wisniewski (Clarion)

Honor Books:

The Graphic Alphabet illustrated and written by David Pelletier (Orchard)

Hush! A Thai Lullaby illustrated by Holly Meade, written by Minfong Ho (Orchard)

The Paperboy illustrated and written by Dav Pilkey (Orchard)

Starry Messenger illustrated and written by Peter Sís (Frances Foster)

1996

Winner:

Officer Buckle and Gloria illustrated and written by Peggy Rathmann (Putnam)

Honor Books:

Tops and Bottoms illustrated and adapted by Janet Stevens (Harcourt)

Zin! Zin! Zin! a Violin illustrated by Marjorie Priceman, written by Lloyd Moss (Simon & Schuster)

Alphabet City illustrated and written by Stephen T. Johnson (Viking)

The Faithful Friend illustrated by Brian Pinkney, written by Robert San Souci (Simon & Schuster)

1995

Winner:

Smoky Night illustrated by David Diaz, written by by Eve Bunting (Harcourt)

Honor Books:

Swamp Angel illustrated by Paul O. Zelinsky, written by Anne Isaacs (Dutton)

Time Flies illustrated and written by Eric Rohmann (Crown)

John Henry illustrated by Jerry Pinkney and text by Julius Lester (Dial)

1994

Winner:

Grandfather's Journey illustrated and written by Allen Say (Houghton)

Honor Books:

Peppe the Lamplighter illustrated by Ted Lewin, written by Elisa Bartone (Lothrop)

In the Small, Small Pond illustrated and written by Denise Fleming (Holt)

Owen illustrated and written by Kevin Henkes (Greenwillow)

Raven: A Trickster Tale from the Pacific Northwest illustrated and written by Gerald McDermott (Harcourt)

Yo! Yes? illustrated and written by Chris Raschka (Orchard)

1993

Winner:

Mirette on the High Wire illustrated and written by Emily McCully (Putnam)

Honor Books

Working Cotton illustrated by Carole Byard , written by Sherley Anne Williams (Harcourt)

Seven Blind Mice illustrated and adapted by Ed Young (Philomel)

The Stinky Cheese Man and Other Fairly Stupid Tales illustrated by Lane Smith, written by Jon Scieszka (Viking)

1992

Winner:

Tuesday illustrated and written by David Wiesner (Clarion)

Honor Book:

Tar Beach illustrated and written by Faith Ringgold (Crown)

1991

Winner:

Black & White illustrated and written by David Macaulay (Houghton)

Honor Books:

"More, More, More," Said the Baby: Three Love Stories illustrated and written by Vera B. Williams (Greenwillow)

Puss in Boots illustrated by Fred Marcellino, text written by Charles Perrault and adapted by Malcolm Arthur (Farrar)

1990

Winner:

Lon Po Po: A Red Riding Hood Story From China illustrated and adapted by Ed Young (Philomel)

Honor Books:

Bill Peet: An Autobiography illustrated and written by Bill Peet (Houghton)

Color Zoo illustrated and written by Lois Ehlert (Lippincott)

Hershel and the Hanukkah Goblins illustrated by Trina Schart Hyman, written by Eric Kimmel (Holiday House)

The Talking Eggs: A Folktale from the American South illustrated by Jerry Pinkney, written by Robert D. San Souci (Dial)

1989

Winner:

Song & Dance Man illustrated by Stephen Gammell, written by Karen Ackerman (Knopf)

Honor Books:

The Boy of the Three-Year Nap illustrated by Allen Say, written by Dianne Snyder (Houghton)

Free Fall illustrated and written by David Wiesner (Lothrop)

Goldilocks and the Three Bears illustrated and written by James Marshall (Dial)

Mirandy and Brother Wind illustrated and written by Patricia C. McKissack (Knopf)

1988
Winner:
Owl Moon illustrated by John Schoenherr, written by Jane Yolen (Philomel)
Honor Book:
Mufaro's Beautiful Daughters: An African Tale illustrated and adapted by John Steptoe (Lothrop)

1987
Winner:
Hey, Al illustrated by Richard Egielski, written by Arthur Yorinks (Farrar)
Honor Books:
Alphabatics illustrated and written by Suse MacDonald (Bradbury)
Rumpelstiltskin illustrated and adapted by Paul O. Zelinsky (Dutton)
The Village of Round and Square Houses illustrated and written by Ann Grifalconi (Little, Brown)

1986
Winner:
Polar Express illustrated and written by Chris Van Allsburg (Houghton)
Honor Books:
King Bidgood's in the Bathtub illustrated by Don Wood, written by Audrey Wood (Harcourt)
The Relatives Came illustrated by Stephen Gammell, written by Cynthia Rylant (Bradbury)

1985
Winner:
Saint George and the Dragon illustrated by Trina Schart. Hyman, adapted by Margaret Hodges (Little, Brown)
Honor Books:
Hansel and Gretel illustrated Paul O. Zelinsky, adapted by Rika Lesser (Dodd)
Have You Seen My Duckling? illustrated and written by Nancy Tafuri (Greenwillow)
The Story of Jumping Mouse: A Native American Legend illustrated and adapted by John Steptoe (Lothrop)

1984
Winner:
The Glorious Flight: Across the Channel with Louis Bleriot illustrated and written by Alice Provensen and Martin Provensen (Viking)
Honor Books:
Little Red Riding Hood illustrated and adapted by Trina Schart Hyman (Holiday House)
Ten, Nine, Eight illustrated and written by Molly Garrett Bang (Greenwillow)

1983
Winner:
Shadow illustrated and text adapted by Marcia Brown (Scribner)
Honor Books:
A Chair for My Mother illustrated and written by Vera B. Williams (Greenwillow)
When I Was Young in the Mountains illustrated by Diane Goode and written by Cynthia Rylant (Dutton)

1982

Winner:

Jumanji illustrated and written by Chris Van Allsburg (Houghton)

Honor Books:

On Market Street illustrated by Anita Lobel, written by Arnold Lobel (Greenwillow)

Outside Over There illustrated and written by Maurice Sendak (Harper)

A Visit to William Blake's Inn: Poems for Innocent and Experienced Travelers illustrated by Alice Provensen and Martin Provensen, written by Nancy Willard (Harcourt)

Where the Buffaloes Begin illustrated by Stephen Gammell, written by Olaf Baker (Warne)

1981

Winner:

Fables illustrated and written by Arnold Lobel (Harper)

Honor Books:

The Bremen-Town Musicians illustrated and adapted by Ilse Plume(Doubleday)

The Grey Lady and the Strawberry Snatcher illustrated and written by Molly Bang (Four Winds)

Mice Twice illustrated and written by Joseph Low (McElderry/Atheneum)

Truck illustrated and written by Donald Crews (Greenwillow)

1980

Winner:

Ox Cart Man illustrated by Barbara Cooney, written by Donald Hall (Viking)

Honor Books:

Ben's Trumpet illustrated and written by Rachel Isadora (Greenwillow)

The Garden of Abdul Gasazi illustrated and written by Chris Van Allsburg (Houghton)

The Treasure illustrated and written by Uri Shulevitz (Farrar)

1979

Winner:

The Girl Who Loved Wild Horses illustrated and written by Paul Goble (Bradbury)

Honor Books:

Freight Train illustrated and written by Donald Crews (Greenwillow)

The Way to Start a Day illustrated by Peter Parnall, written by Byrd Baylor (Scribner)

1978

Winner:

Noah's Ark illustrated and adapted by Peter Spier (Doubleday)

Honor Books:

Castle illustrated and written by David Macaulay (Houghton)

It Could Always Be Worse illustrated and adapted by Margot Zemach (Farrar)

1977

Winner:

Ashanti to Zulu: African Traditions illustrated by Leo and Diane Dillon, written by Margaret W. Musgrove
 (Dial)

Honor Books:

The Amazing Bone illustrated and written by William Steig (Farrar)

The Contest illustrated and adapted by Nonny Hogrogian (Greenwillow)

Fish For Supper illustrated and written by M. B. Goffstein (Dial)

The Golem: A Jewish Legend illustrated and written by Beverly Brodsky McDermott (Lippincott)

Hawk, I'm Your Brother illustrated by Peter Parnell, written by Byrd Baylor (Scribner)

1976

Winner:

Why Mosquitoes Buzz in People's Ears: A West African Tale illustrated by Leo and Diane Dillon,
 adapted by Verna Aardema (Dial)

Honor Books:

The Desert Is Theirs illustrated by Peter Parnall, written by Byrd Baylor (Scribner)

Strega Nona illustrated and written by Tomie de Paola (Prentice-Hall)

1975

Winner:

Arrow to the Sun: A Pueblo Indian Tale illustrated and adapted by Gerald McDermott (Viking)

Honor Book:

Jambo Means Hello: A Swahili Alphabet Book illustrated by Tom Feelings, written by Muriel Feelings
 (Dial)

1974

Winner:

Duffy and the Devil illustrated by Maragaer Zemach, adapted by Harve Zemach (Farrar)

Honor Books:

Cathedral illustrated and written by David Macaulay (Houghton)

Three Jovial Huntsmen illustrated and written by Susan Jeffers (Bradbury)

1973

Winner:

The Funny Little Woman illustrated by Blair Lent, written by Arlene Mosel (Dutton)

Honor Books:

Anansi the Spider: A Tale from the Ashanti illustrated and adapted by Gerald McDermott (Holt)

Hosie's Alphabet illustrated by Leonard Baskin, written by Hosea, Tobias and Lisa Baskin (Viking)

Snow-White and the Seven Dwarfs illustrated by Nancy Eckholm Burkert, adapted from Brothers Grimm
 by Randall Jarrell (Farrar)

When Clay Sings illustrated by Tom Bahti, written by Byrd Baylor (Scribner)

1972
Winner:
One Fine Day illustrated and adapted by Nonny Hogrogian (Macmillan)
Honor Books:
Hildilid's Night illustrated by Arnold Lobel, written by Cheli Duran Ryan (Macmillan)
If All the Seas Were One Sea illustrated and written by Janina Domanska (Macmillan)
Moja Means One: A Swahili Counting Book illustrated by Tom Feelings, written by Muriel Feelings
   (Dial)

1971
Winner:
A Story, a Story: An African Tale illustrated and adapted by Gail E. Haley (Atheneum)
Honor Books:
The Angry Moon illustrated by Blair Lent, adapted by William Sleator (Atlantic)
Frog and Toad Are Friends illustrated and written by Arnold Lobel (Harper)
In the Night Kitchen illustrated and written by Maurice Sendak (Harper)

1970
Winner:
Sylvester and the Magic Pebble illustrated and written by William Steig (Windmill)
Honor Books:
Alexander and the Wind-up Mouse illustrated and written by Leo Lionni (Pantheon)
Goggles! illustrated and written by Ezra Jack Keats (Macmillan)
The Judge: An Untrue Tale illustrated by Margot Zemach, written by Harve Zemach (Farrar)
Pop Corn & Ma Goodness illustrated by Robert Andrew Parker, written by Edna Mitchell Preston
   (Viking)
Thy Friend, Obadiah illustrated and written by Brinton Turkle (Viking)

1969
Winner:
The Fool of the World and the Flying Ship illustrated by Uri Shulevitz, adapted by Arthur Ransome
   (Farrar)
Honor Book:
Why the Sun and the Moon Live in the Sky illustrated by Blair Lent, written by by Elphinstone Dayrell
   (Houghton)

1968
Winner:
Drummer Hoff illustrated by Ed Emberley, adapted by Barbara Emberley (Prentice-Hall)
Honor Books:
The Emperor and the Kite illustrated by Ed Young, written by Jane Yolen (World)
Frederick illustrated and written by Leo Lionni (Pantheon)
Seashore Story illustrated and written by Taro Yashima (Viking)

1967
Winner:
Sam, Bangs, and Moonshine illustrated and written by Evaline Ness (Holt)
Honor Book:
One Wide River to Cross illustrated by Ed Emberley, adapted by Barbara Emberley (Prentice-Hall)

1966
Winner:
Always Room for One More illustrated by Nonny Hogrogian, written by Sorche Nic Leodhas (Holt)
Honor Books:
Hide and Seek Fog illustrated by Roger Duvoisin, written by Alvin Tresselt (Lothrop)
Just Me illustrated and written by Marie Hall Ets (Viking)
Tom Tit Tot illustrated and adapted by Evaline Ness (Scribner)

1965
Winner:
May I Bring a Friend? illustrated by Beni Montresor, written by Beatrice Schenk De Regniers (Atheneum)
Honor Books:
A Pocketful of Cricket illustrated by Evaline Ness, written by Rebecca Caudill (Holt)
Rain Makes Applesauce illustrated by Marvin Bileck, wiritten by Julian Scheer (Holiday)
The Wave illustrated by Blair Lent, written by Margaret Hodges (Houghton)

1964
Winner:
Where the Wild Things Are illustrated and written by Maurice Sendak (Harper)
Honor Books:
All in the Morning Early illustrated by Evaline Ness, written by Sorche Nic Leodhas (Holt)
Mother Goose & Nursery Rhymes illustrated and adapted by Phillip Reed (Atheneum)
Swimmy illustrated and written by Leo Lionni (Pantheon)

1963
Winner:
Snowy Day illustrated and written by Ezra Jack Keats (Viking)
Honor Books:
Mr. Rabbit and the Lovely Present illustrated by Maurice Sendak, written by Charlotte Zolotow (Harper)
The Sun Is a Golden Earring illustrated by Bernarda Bryson, written by Natalia M. Belting (Holt)

1962
Winner:
Once a Mouse illustrated and adapted by Marcia Brown (Scribner)
Honor Books:
The Day We Saw the Sun Come Up illustrated by Adrienne Adams, written by Alice E. Goudey (Scribner)
The Fox Went Out on a Chilly Night: An Old Song illustrated and adapted by Peter Spier (Doubleday)
Little Bear's Visit illustrated by Maurice Sendak, written by Else Holmelund Minarik (Harper)

1961
Winner:
Baboushka and the Three Kings illustrated by Nicolas Sidjakov, written by Ruth Robbins (Parnassus)
Honor Book:
Inch by Inch illustrated and written by Leo Lionni (Obolensky)

1960
Winner:
Nine Days to Christmas illustrated by Marie Hall Ets, written by Marie Hall Ets and Aurora Labastida (Viking)
Honor Books:
Houses from the Sea illustrated by Adrienne Adams, written by Alice E. Goudey (Scribner)
The Moon Jumpers illustrated by Maurice Sendak, written by Janice May Udry (Harper)

1959
Winner:
Chanticleer and the Fox illustrated and adapted (from Chaucer) by Barbara Cooney (Crowell)
Honor Books:
The House That Jack Built: La Maison Que Jacques A Batie illustrated and adapted by Antonio Frasconi (Harcourt)
Umbrella illustrated and written by Taro Yashima (Viking)
What Do You Say, Dear? illustrated by Maurice Sendak, written by Sesyle Joslin (W.R. Scott)

1958
Winner:
Time of Wonder illustrated and written by Robert McCloskey (Viking)
Honor Books:
Anatole and the Cat illustrated by Paul Galdone, written by Eve Titus (McGraw-Hill)
Fly High, Fly Low illustrated and written by Don Freeman (Viking)

1957
Winner:
Tree Is Nice illustrated by Marc Simont, written by Janice May Udry (Harper)
Honor Books:
Anatole illustrated by Paul Galdone, written by Eve Titus (McGraw-Hill)
Gillespie and the Guards illustrated by James Daugherty, written by Benjamin Elkin (Viking)
Lion illustrated and written by William Pène du Bois (Viking)
Mr. Penny's Race Horse illustrated and written by Marie Hall Ets (Viking)
1 Is One illustrated and written by Tasha Tudor (Walck)

1956

Winner:

Frog Went A-Courtin' illustrated by Feodor Rojankovsky, adapted by John Langstaff (Harcourt)

Honor Books:

Crow Boy illustrated and written by Taro Yashima (Viking)

Play with Me illustrated and written by Marie Hall Ets (Viking)

1955

Winner:

Cinderella, or The Little Glass Slipper illustrated and adapted from Perrault by Marcia Brown (Scribner)

Honor Books:

Book of Nursery and Mother Goose Rhymes illustrated by Marguerite de Angeli (Doubleday)

The Thanksgiving Story illustrated by Helen Sewell, written by Alice Dalgliesh (Scribner)

Wheel on the Chimney illustrated by Tibor Gergely, written by Margaret Wise Brown (Lippincott)

1954

Winner:

Madeline's Rescue illustrated and written by Ludwig Bemelmans (Viking)

Honor Books:

A Very Special House illustrated by Maurice Sendak, written by Ruth Krauss (Harper)

Green Eyes illustrated and written by A. Birnbaum (Capitol)

Journey Cake, Ho! illustrated by Robert McCloskey, written by by Ruth Sawyer (Viking)

The Steadfast Tin Soldier illustrated by Marcia Brown, adapted by M.R. James (Scribner)

When Will the World Be Mine? illustrated by Jean Charlot, written by Miriam Schlein (W. R. Scott)

1953

Winner:

The Biggest Bear illustrated and written by Lynd Kendall Ward (Houghton)

Honor Books:

Ape in a Cape: An Alphabet Of Odd Animals illustrated and written by Fritz Eichenberg (Harcourt)

Five Little Monkeys illustrated and written by Juliet Kepes (Houghton)

One Morning in Maine illustrated and written by Robert McCloskey (Viking)

Puss in Boots illustrated and adapted from Perrault by Marcia Brown (Scribner)

The Storm Book by illustrated by Margaret Bloy Graham, written by Charlotte Zolotow (Harper)

1952

Winner:

Finders Keepers illustrated by Nicolas Mordvinoff, written by William Lipkind (Harcourt)

Honor Books:

All Falling Down illustrated by Margaret Bloy Graham, written by Gene Zion (Harper)

Bear Party illustrated and written by William Péne du Bois (Viking)

Feather Mountain illustrated and written by Elizabeth Olds (Houghton)

Mr. T.W. Anthony Woo illustrated and written by Marie Hall Ets (Viking)

Skipper John's Cook illustrated and written by Marcia Brown (Scribner)

1951

Winner:

The Egg Tree illustrated and written by Katherine Milhous (Scribner)

Honor Books:

Dick Whittington and His Cat illustrated and adapted by Marcia Brown (Scribner)

If I Ran the Zoo illustrated and written by Dr. Seuss (Random House)

The Most Wonderful Doll in the World illustrated by Helen Stone, written by Phyllis McGinley (Lippincott)

T-Bone, the Baby Sitter illustrated and written by Clare Newberry (Harper)

The Two Reds illustrated by Nicholas Mordvinoff, written by William Lipkind (Harcourt)

1950

Winner:

Song of the Swallows illustrated and written by Leo Politi (Scribner)

Honor Books:

America's Ethan Allen illustrated by Lynd Ward, written by Stewart Holbrook (Houghton)

Bartholomew and the Oobleck illustrated and written by Dr. Seuss (Random House)

The Happy Day illustrated by Marc Simont, written by Ruth Krauss (Harper)

Henry Fisherman illustrated and written by Marcia Brown (Scribner)

The Wild Birthday Cake illustrated by Hildegard Woodward, written by Lavinia Davis (Doubleday)

1949

Winner:

The Big Snow illustrated and written by Berta and Elmer Hader (Macmillan)

Honor Books:

All Around the Town illustrated by Helen Stone, written by Phyllis McGinley (Lippincott)

Blueberries for Sal illustrated and written by Robert McCloskey (Viking)

Fish in the Air illustrated and written by Kurt Wiese (Viking)

Juanita illustrated and written by Leo Politi (Scribner)

1948

Winner:

White Snow, Bright Snow illustrated by Roger Duvoisin, written by Alvin Tresselt (Lothrop)

Honor Books:

Bambino the Clown illustrated and written by George S. Schreiber (Viking)

McElligot's Pool illustrated and written by Dr. Seuss (Random House)

Roger and the Fox illustrated by Hildegard Woodward, written by Lavinia Davis (Doubleday)

Song of Robin Hood illustrated by Virginia Lee Burton, edited by Anne Malcolmson (Houghton)

Stone Soup illustrated and written by Marcia Brown (Scribner)

1947

Winner:

The Little Island illustrated by Leonard Weisgard, written by Golden MacDonald (Doubleday)

Honor Books:

Boats on the River illustrated by Jay Hyde Barnum, written by Marjorie Flack (Viking)

Pedro, the Angel of Olvera Street illustrated and written by Leo Politi (Scribner)

Rain Drop Splash illustrated by Leonard Weisgard, written by Alvin Tresselt (Lothrop)

Sing in Praise: A Collection of the Best Loved Hymns illustrated by Marjorie Torrey, text selected by Opal Wheeler (Dutton)

Timothy Turtle illustrated by Tony Palazzo, written by Al Graham (Welch)

1946

Winner:

The Rooster Crows illustrated and written by Miska Petersham and Maud Petersham (Macmillan)

Honor Books:

Little Lost Lamb illustrated by Leonard Weisgard, written by Golden MacDonald (Doubleday)

My Mother Is the Most Beautiful Woman in the World illustrated by Ruth C. Gannett, written by Becky Reyher (Lothrop)

Sing Mother Goose illustrated by Marjorie Torrey, music by Opal Wheeler (Dutton)

You Can Write Chinese illustrated and written by Kurt Wiese (Viking)

1945

Winner:

Prayer for a Child by Rachel L. Field and Elizabeth Orton Jones

Honor Books:

The Christmas Anna Angel illustrated by Kate Seredy, written by Ruth Sawyer (Viking)

In the Forest illustrated and written by Marie Hall Ets (Viking)

Mother Goose illustrated by Tasha Tudor (Oxford University Press)

Yonie Wondernose illustrated and written by Marguerite de Angeli (Doubleday)

1944

Winner:

Many Moons illustrated by Louis Slobodkin, written by James Thurber (Harcourt)

Honor Books:

A Child's Good Night Book illustrated by Jean Charlot, written by Margaret Wise Brown (W. R. Scott)

Good Luck Horse illustrated by Plato Chan, written by Chin-Yi Chan (Whittlesey)

The Mighty Hunter illustrated and written by Berta and Elmer Hader (Macmillan)

Pierre Pigeon illustrated by Arnold E. Bare, written by Lee Kingman (Houghton)

Small Rain: Verses from the Bible illustrated by Elizabeth Orton Jones, text selected by Jessie Orton Jones (Viking)

1943

Winner:

The Little House illustrated and written by Virginia Lee Burton (Houghton)

Honor Books:

Dash and Dart illustrated and written by Mary and Conrad Buff (Viking)

Marshmallow illustrated and written by Clare Turlay Newberry (Harper)

1942

Winner:

Make Way for Ducklings illustrated and written by Robert McCloskey (Viking)

Honor Books:

An American ABC by Maud Petersham and Miska Petersham (Macmillan)

In My Mother's House illustrated by Velino Herrera, written by Ann Nolan Clark (Viking)

Nothing at All illustrated and written by Wanda Gág (Coward)

Paddle-to-the-Sea illustrated and written by Holling C. Holling (Houghton)

1941

Winner:

They Were Strong and Good illustrated and written by Robert Lawson (Viking)

Honor Book:

April's Kittens illustrated and written by Claire Newberry (Harper)

1940

Winner:

Abraham Lincoln illustrated by Edgar Parin D'Aulaire, written by Ingri D'Aulaire (Doubleday)

Honor Books:

The Ageless Story illustrated and written by Lauren Ford (Dodd)

Cock-A-Doodle Doo by Berta and Elmer Hader (Macmillan)

Madeline illustrated and written by Ludwig Bemelmans (Viking)

1939

Winner:

Mei Li illustrated and written by Thomas Handforth (Doubleday)

Honor Books:

Andy and the Lion illustrated and written by James Daugherty (Viking)

Barkis illustrated and written by Clare Newberry (Harper)

The Forest Pool illustrated and written by Laura Adams Armer (Longmans)

Snow White and the Seven Dwarfs illustrated and written by Wanda Gág (Coward)

Wee Gillis illustrated by Robert Lawson, written by Munro Leaf (Viking)

1938

Winner:

Animals of the Bible illustrated by Dorothy P. Lathrop, adapted by Helen D. Fish (Lippincott)

Honor Books:

Four and Twenty Blackbirds illustrated by Robert Lawson, adapted by Helen D. Fish (Stokes)

Seven Simeons: A Russian Tale illustrated and adapted by Boris Artzybasheff (Viking)

NEWBERY MEDAL WINNERS AND HONOR BOOKS
1922–2001

The Newbery Medal honors the year's most distinguished contribution to American literature for children. The medal was established in 1922 and is presented annually by the Association for Library Service to Children (ALSC), a division of the American Library Association (ALA). The recipient must be a citizen or resident of the United States.

2001
Winner:
A Year Down Yonder by Richard Peck (Dial)
Honor Books:
Because of Winn-Dixie by Kate DiCamillo (Candlewick)
Hope Was Here by Joan Bauer (G.P. Putnam's Sons)
Joey Pigza Loses Control by Jack Gantos (Farrar, Strauss, Giroux)
The Wanderer by Sharon Creech (HarperCollins)

2000
Winner:
Bud, Not Buddy by Christopher Paul Curtis (Delacorte)
Honor Books:
Getting Near to Baby by Audrey Couloumbis (G. P. Putnam's Sons)
26 Fairmount Avenue by Tomie dePaola (G. P. Putnam's Sons)
Our Only May Amelia by Jennifer L. Holm (HarperCollins)

1999
Winner:
Holes by Louis Sachar (Frances Foster)
Honor Book:
A Long Way from Chicago by Richard Peck (Dial)

1998
Winner:
Out of the Dust by Karen Hesse (Scholastic)
Honor Books:
Ella Enchanted by Gail Carson Levine (HarperCollins)
Lily's Crossing by Patricia Reilly Giff (Delacorte)
Wringer by Jerry Spinelli (HarperCollins)

1997
Winner:
The View from Saturday by E.L. Konigsburg (Atheneum)
Honor Books:
A Girl Named Disaster by Nancy Farmer (Orchard)
Moorchild by Eloise McGraw (McElderry)
The Thief by Megan Whalen Turner (Greenwillow)
Belle Prater's Boy by Ruth White (Farrar, Strauss, Giroux)

1996
Winner:
The Midwife's Apprentice by Karen Cushman (Clarion)
Honor Books:
What Jamie Saw by Carolyn Coman (Front Street)
The Watsons Go to Birmingham: 1963 by Christopher Paul Curtis (Delacorte)
Yolonda's Genius by Carol Fenner (McElderry)
The Great Fire by Jim Murphy (Scholastic)

1995
Winner:
Walk Two Moons by Sharon Creech (HarperCollins)
Honor Books:
Catherine, Called Birdy by Karen Cushman (Clarion)
The Ear, the Eye and the Arm by Nancy Farmer (Orchard)

1994
Winner:
The Giver by Lois Lowry (Houghton)
Honor Books:
Crazy Lady by Jane Leslie Conly (HarperCollins)
Dragon's Gate by Laurence Yep (HarperCollins)
Eleanor Roosevelt: A Life of Discovery by Russell Freedman (Clarion)

1993
Winner:
Missing May by Cynthia Rylant (Orchard)
Honor Books:
What Hearts by Bruce Brooks (HarperCollins)
The Dark-Thirty: Southern Tales of the Supernatural by Patricia McKissack (Knopf)
Somewhere in the Darkness by Walter Dean Myers (Scholastic)

1992
Winner:
Shiloh by Phyllis Reynolds Naylor (Atheneum)
Honor Books:
Nothing but the Truth: A Documentary Novel by Avi (Orchard)
The Wright Brothers: How They Invented the Airplane by Russell Freedman (Holiday House)

1991

Winner:

Maniac Magee by Jerry Spinelli (Little, Brown)

Honor Book:

The True Confessions of Charlotte Doyle by Avi (Orchard)

1990

Winner:

Number the Stars by Lois Lowry (Houghton)

Honor Books:

Afternoon of the Elves by Janet Taylor Lisle (Orchard)

Shabanu, Daughter of the Wind by Suzanne Fisher Staples (Knopf)

The Winter Room by Gary Paulsen (Orchard)

1989

Winner:

Joyful Noise: Poems of Two Voices by Paul Fleischman (Harper)

Honor Books:

In the Beginning: Creation Stories from Around the World by Virginia Hamilton (Harcourt)

Scorpions by Walter Dean Myers (Harper)

1988

Winner:

Lincoln: A Photobiography by Russell Freedman (Clarion)

Honor Books:

After the Rain by Norma Fox Mazer (Morrow)

Hatchet by Gary Paulsen (Bradbury)

1987

Winner:

The Whipping Boy by Sid Fleischman (Greenwillow)

Honor Books:

A Fine White Dust by Cynthia Rylant (Bradbury)

On My Honor by Marion Dane Bauer (Clarion)

Volcano: The Eruption and Healing of Mount St. Helens by Patricia Lauber (Bradbury)

1986

Winner:

Sarah, Plain and Tall by Patricia MacLachlan (Harper)

Honor Books:

Commodore Perry in the Land of the Shogun by Rhoda Blumberg (Lothrop)

Dogsong by Gary Paulsen (Bradbury)

1985
Winner:
The Hero and the Crown by Robin McKinley (Greenwillow)
Honor Books:
Like Jake and Me by Mavis Jukes (Knopf)
The Moves Make the Man by Bruce Brooks (Harper)
One-Eyed Cat by Paula Fox (Bradbury)

1984
Winner:
Dear Mr. Henshaw by Beverly Cleary (Morrow)
Honor Books:
The Sign of the Beaver by Elizabeth George Speare (Houghton)
A Solitary Blue by Cynthia Voigt (Atheneum)
Sugaring Time by Kathryn Lasky (Macmillan)
The Wish Giver: Three Tales of Coven Tree by Bill Brittain (Harper)

1983
Winner:
Dicey's Song by Cynthia Voigt (Atheneum)
Honor Books:
The Blue Sword by Robin McKinley (Greenwillow)
Doctor De Soto by William Steig (Farrar)
Graven Images by Paul Fleischman (Harper)
Homesick: My Own Story by Jean Fritz (Putnam)
Sweet Whispers, Brother Rush by Virginia Hamilton (Philomel)

1982
Winner:
A Visit to William Blake's Inn: Poems for Innocent and Experienced Travelers by Nancy Willard (Harcourt)
Honor Books:
Ramona Quimby, Age 8 by Beverly Cleary (Morrow)
Upon the Head of the Goat: A Childhood in Hungary 1939-1944 by Aranka Siegal (Farrar)

1981
Winner:
Jacob Have I Loved by Katherine Paterson (Crowell)
Honor Books:
The Fledgling by Jane Langton (Harper)
A Ring of Endless Light by Madeleine L'Engle (Farrar)

1980
Winner:
A Gathering of Days: A New England Girl's Journal, 1830-32 by Joan Blos (Scribner)
Honor Book:
The Road from Home: The Story of an Armenian Girl by David Kherdian (Greenwillow)

1979
Winner:
The Westing Game by Ellen Raskin (Dutton)
Honor Book:
The Great Gilly Hopkins by Katherine Paterson (Crowell)

1978
Winner:
Bridge to Terabithia by Katherine Paterson (Crowell)
Honor Books:
Ramona and Her Father by Beverly Cleary (Morrow)
Anpao: An American Indian Odyssey by Jamake Highwater (Lippincott)

1977
Winner:
Roll of Thunder, Hear My Cry by Mildred Taylor (Dial)
Honor Books:
Abel's Island by William Steig (Farrar)
A String in the Harp by Nancy Bond (Atheneum)

1976
Winner:
The Grey King by Susan Cooper (McElderry)
Honor Books:
The Hundred Penny Box by Sharon Bell Mathis (Viking)
Dragonwings by Laurence Yep (Harper)

1975
Winner:
M. C. Higgins, the Great by Virginia Hamilton (Macmillan)
Honor Books:
Figgs and Phantoms by Ellen Raskin (Dutton)
My Brother Sam Is Dead by James Lincoln Collier and Christopher Collier (Four Winds)
The Perilous Gard by Elizabeth Marie Pope (Houghton)
Philip Hall Likes Me, I Reckon Maybe by Bette Greene (Dial)

1974
Winner:
The Slave Dancer by Paula Fox (Bradbury)
Honor Book:
The Dark Is Rising by Susan Cooper (McElderry)

1973
Winner:
Julie of the Wolves by Jean Craighead George (Harper)
Honor Books:
Frog and Toad Together by Arnold Lobel (Harper)
The Upstairs Room by Johanna Reiss (Crowell)
The Witches of Worm by Zilpha Keatley Snyder (Atheneum)

1972
Winner:
Mrs. Frisby and the Rats of NIMH by Robert C. O'Brien (Atheneum)
Honor Books:
Incident at Hawk's Hill by Allan W. Eckert (Little, Brown)
The Planet of Junior Brown by Virginia Hamilton (Macmillan)
The Tombs of Atuan by Ursula K. Le Guin (Atheneum)
Annie and the Old One by Miska Miles (Little, Brown)
The Headless Cupid by Zilpha Keatley Snyder (Atheneum)

1971
Winner:
Summer of the Swans by Betsy Byars (Viking)
Honor Books:
Knee Knock Rise by Natalie Babbitt (Farrar)
Enchantress from the Stars by Sylvia Louise Engdahl (Atheneum)
Sing Down the Moon by Scott O'Dell (Houghton)

1970
Winner:
Sounder by William H. Armstrong (Harper)
Honor Books:
Our Eddie by Sulamith Ish-Kishor (Pantheon)
The Many Ways of Seeing: An Introduction to the Pleasures of Art by Janet Gaylord Moore (World)
Journey Outside by Mary Q. Steele (Viking)

1969
Winner:
The High King by Lloyd Alexander (Holt)
Honor Books:
To Be a Slave by Julius Lester (Dial)
When Shlemiel Went to Warsaw and Other Stories by Isaac Bashevis Singer (Farrar)

1968
Winner:
From the Mixed-Up Files of Mrs. Basil E. Frankweiler by E. L. Konigsburg (Atheneum)
Honor Books:
Jennifer, Hecate, Macbeth, William McKinley, and Me, Elizabeth by E. L. Konigsburg (Atheneum)
The Black Pearl by Scott O'Dell (Houghton)
The Fearsome Inn by Isaac Bashevis Singer (Scribner)
The Egypt Game by Zilpha Keatley Snyder (Atheneum)

1967
Winner:
Up a Road Slowly by Irene Hunt (Follett)
Honor Books:
The King's Fifth by Scott O'Dell (Houghton)
Zlateh the Goat and Other Stories by Isaac Bashevis Singer (Harper)
The Jazz Man by Mary Hays Weik (Atheneum)

1966
Winner:
I, Juan de Pareja by Elizabeth Borton de Treviño (Farrar)
Honor Books:
The Black Cauldron by Lloyd Alexander (Holt)
The Animal Family by Randall Jarrell (Pantheon)
The Noonday Friends by Mary Stolz (Harper)

1965
Winner:
Shadow of a Bull by Maia Wojciechowska (Atheneum)
Honor Book:
Across Five Aprils by Irene Hunt (Follett)

1964
Winner:
It's Like This, Cat by Emily Cheney Neville (Harper)
Honor Books:
Rascal: A Memoir of a Better Era by Sterling North (Dutton)
The Loner by Ester Wier (McKay)

1963
Winner:
A Wrinkle in Time by Madeleine L'Engle (Farrar)
Honor Books:
Thistle and Thyme: Tales and Legends from Scotland by Sorche Nic Leodhas (Holt)
Men of Athens by Olivia Coolidge (Houghton)

1962
Winner:
The Bronze Bow by Elizabeth George Speare (Houghton)
Honor Books:
Frontier Living by Edwin Tunis (World)
The Golden Goblet by Eloise Jarvis McGraw (Coward)
Belling the Tiger by Mary Stolz (Harper)

1961
Winner:
Island of the Blue Dolphins by Scott O'Dell (Houghton)
Honor Books:
America Moves Forward: A History for Peter by Gerald W. Johnson (Morrow)
Old Ramon by Jack Schaefer (Houghton)
The Cricket in Times Square by George Selden, pseud. George Thompson (Farrar)

1960

Winner:

Onion John by Joseph Krumgold (Crowell)

Honor Books:

My Side of the Mountain by Jean Craighead George (Dutton)

America Is Born: A History for Peter by Gerald Johnson (Morrow)

The Gammage Cup by Carol Kendall (Harcourt)

1959

Winner:

The Witch of Blackbird Pond by Elizabeth George Speare (Houghton)

Honor Books:

The Family Under the Bridge by Natalie Savage Carlson (Harper)

Along Came a Dog by Meindert DeJong (Harper)

Chucaro: Wild Pony of the Pampa by Francis Kalnay (Harcourt)

The Perilous Road by William O. Steele (Harcourt)

1958

Winner:

Rifles for Watie by Harold Keith (Crowell)

Honor Books:

The Horsecatcher by Mari Sandoz (Westminster)

Gone-Away Lake by Elizabeth Enright (Harcourt)

The Great Wheel by Robert Lawson (Viking)

Tom Paine, Freedom's Apostle by Leo Gurko (Crowell)

1957

Winner:

Miracles on Maple Hill by Virginia Sorensen (Harcourt)

Honor Books:

Old Yeller by Fred Gipson (Harper)

The House of Sixty Fathers by Meindert DeJong (Harper)

Mr. Justice Holmes by Clara Ingram Judson (Follett)

The Corn Grows Ripe by Dorothy Rhoads (Viking)

Black Fox of Lorne by Marguerite de Angeli (Doubleday)

1956

Winner:

Carry On, Mr. Bowditch by Jean Lee Latham (Houghton)

Honor Books:

The Secret River by Marjorie Kinnan Rawlings (Scribner)

The Golden Name Day by Jennie Lindquist (Harper)

Men, Microscopes, and Living Things by Katherine Shippen (Viking)

1955
Winner:
The Wheel on the School by Meindert DeJong (Harper)
Honor Books:
Courage of Sarah Noble by Alice Dalgliesh (Scribner)
Banner in the Sky by James Ullman (Lippincott)

1954
Winner:
...And Now Miguel by Joseph Krumgold (Crowell)
Honor Books:
All Alone by Claire H. Bishop (Viking)
Shadrach by Meindert DeJong (Harper)
Hurry Home, Candy by Meindert DeJong (Harper)
Theodore Roosevelt, Fighting Patriot by Clara Ingram Judson (Follett)
Magic Maize by Mary and Conrad Buff (Houghton)

1953
Winner:
Secret of the Andes by Ann Nolan Clark (Viking)
Honor Books:
Charlotte's Web by E. B. White (Harper)
Moccasin Trail by Eloise Jarvis McGraw (Coward)
Red Sails to Capri by Ann Weil (Viking)
The Bears on Hemlock Mountain by Alice Dalgliesh (Scribner)
Birthdays of Freedom, Vol. 1 by Genevieve Foster (Scribner)

1952
Winner:
Ginger Pye by Eleanor Estes (Harcourt)
Honor Books:
Americans Before Columbus by Elizabeth Baity (Viking)
Minn of the Mississippi by Holling C. Holling (Houghton)
The Defender by Nicholas Kalashnikoff (Scribner)
The Light at Tern Rock by Julia Sauer (Viking)
The Apple and the Arrow by Mary and Conrad Buff (Houghton)

1951
Winner:
Amos Fortune, Free Man by Elizabeth Yates (Dutton)
Honor Books:
Better Known as Johnny Appleseed by Mabel Leigh Hunt (Lippincott)
Gandhi, Fighter Without a Sword by Jeanette Eaton (Morrow)
Abraham Lincoln, Friend of the People by Clara Ingram Judson (Follett)
The Story of Appleby Capple by Anne Parrish (Harper)

1950
Winner:
The Door in the Wall by Marguerite de Angeli (Doubleday)
Honor Books:
Tree of Freedom by Rebecca Caudill (Viking)
The Blue Cat of Castle Town by Catherine Coblentz (Longmans)
Kildee House by Rutherford Montgomery (Doubleday)
George Washington by Genevieve Foster (Scribner)
Song of the Pines: A Story of Norwegian Lumbering in Wisconsin by Walter and Marion Havighurst (Winston)

1949
Winner:
King of the Wind by Marguerite Henry (Rand McNally)
Honor Books:
Seabird by Holling C. Holling (Houghton)
Daughter of the Mountains by Louise Rankin (Viking)
My Father's Dragon by Ruth S. Gannett (Random House)
Story of the Negro by Arna Bontemps (Knopf)

1948
Winner:
The Twenty-One Balloons by William Pène du Bois (Viking)
Honor Books:
Pancakes-Paris by Claire H. Bishop (Viking)
Li Lun, Lad of Courage by Carolyn Treffinger (Abingdon)
The Quaint and Curious Quest of Johnny Longfoot by Catherine Besterman (Bobbs-Merrill)
The Cow-Tail Switch, and Other West African Stories by Harold Courlander (Holt)
Misty of Chincoteague by Marguerite Henry (Rand McNally)

1947
Winner:
Miss Hickory by Carolyn Sherwin Bailey (Viking)
Honor Books:
Wonderful Year by Nancy Barnes (Messner)
Big Tree by Mary and Conrad Buff (Viking)
The Heavenly Tenants by William Maxwell (Harper)
The Avion My Uncle Flew by Cyrus Fisher (Appleton)
The Hidden Treasure of Glaston by Eleanor Jewett (Viking)

1946
Winner:
Strawberry Girl by Lois Lenski (Lippincott)
Honor Books:
Justin Morgan Had a Horse by Marguerite Henry (Rand McNally)
The Moved-Outers by Florence Crannell Means (Houghton)
Bhimsa, the Dancing Bear by Christine Weston (Scribner)
New Found World by Katherine Shippen (Viking)

1945
Winner:
Rabbit Hill by Robert Lawson (Viking)
Honor Books:
The Hundred Dresses by Eleanor Estes (Harcourt)
The Silver Pencil by Alice Dalgliesh (Scribner)
Abraham Lincoln's World by Genevieve Foster (Scribner)
Lone Journey: The Life of Roger Williams by Jeanette Eaton (Harcourt)

1944
Winner:
Johnny Tremain by Esther Forbes (Houghton)
Honor Books:
These Happy Golden Years by Laura Ingalls Wilder (Harper)
Fog Magic by Julia Sauer (Viking)
Rufus M. by Eleanor Estes (Harcourt)
Mountain Born by Elizabeth Yates (Coward)

1943
Winner:
Adam of the Road by Elizabeth Janet Gray (Viking)
Honor Books:
The Middle Moffat by Eleanor Estes (Harcourt)
Have You Seen Tom Thumb by Mabel Leigh Hunt (Lippincott)

1942
Winner:
The Matchlock Gun by Walter D. Edmonds (Dodd)
Honor Books:
Little Town on the Prairie by Laura Ingalls Wilder (Harper)
George Washington's World by Genevieve Foster (Scribner)
Indian Captive: The Story of Mary Jemison by Lois Lenski (Lippincott)
Down Ryton Water by Eva Roe Gaggin (Viking)

1941
Winner:
Call It Courage by Armstrong Sperry (Macmillan)
Honor Books:
Blue Willow by Doris Gates (Viking)
Young Mac of Fort Vancouver by Mary Jane Carr (Crowell)
The Long Winter by Laura Ingalls Wilder (Harper)
Nansen by Anna Gertrude Hall (Viking)

1940

Winner:

Daniel Boone by James Daugherty (Viking)

Honor Books:

The Singing Tree by Kate Seredy (Viking)

Runner of the Mountain Tops: The Life of Louis Agassiz by Mabel Robinson (Random House)

By the Shores of Silver Lake by Laura Ingalls Wilder (Harper)

Boy With a Pack by Stephen W. Meader (Harcourt)

1939

Winner:

Thimble Summer by Elizabeth Enright (Rinehart)

Honor Books:

Nino by Valenti Angelo (Viking)

Mr. Popper's Penguins by Richard and Florence Atwater (Little, Brown)

Hello the Boat! by Phyllis Crawford (Holt)

Leader by Destiny: George Washington, Man and Patriot by Jeanette Eaton (Harcourt)

Penn by Elizabeth Janet Gray (Viking)

1938

Winner:

The White Stag by Kate Seredy (Viking)

Honor Books:

Pecos Bill by James Cloyd Bowman (Little, Brown)

Bright Island by Mabel Robinson (Random House)

On the Banks of Plum Creek by Laura Ingalls Wilder (Harper)

1937

Winner:

Roller Skates by Ruth Sawyer (Viking)

Honor Books:

Phebe Fairchild: Her Book by Lois Lenski (Stokes)

Whistler's Van by Idwal Jones (Viking)

The Golden Basket by Ludwig Bemelmans (Viking)

Winterbound by Margery Bianco (Viking)

The Codfish Musket by Agnes Hewes (Doubleday)

Audubon by Constance Rourke (Harcourt)

1936

Winner:

Caddie Woodlawn by Carol Ryrie Brink (Macmillan)

Honor Books:

Honk, the Moose by Phil Strong (Dodd)

The Good Master by Kate Seredy (Viking)

Young Walter Scott by Elizabeth Janet Gray (Viking)

All Sail Set: A Romance of the Flying Cloud by Armstrong Sperry (Winston)

1935
Winner:
Dobry by Monica Shannon (Viking)
Honor Books:
Pageant of Chinese History by Elizabeth Seeger (Longmans)
Davy Crockett by Constance Rourke (Harcourt)
Day on Skates: The Story of a Dutch Picnic by Hilda von Stockum (Harper)

1934
Winner:
Invincible Louisa: The Story of the Author of Little Women by Cornelia Meigs (Little, Brown)
Honor Books:
The Forgotten Daughter by Caroline Snedeker (Doubleday)
Swords of Steel by Elsie Singmaster (Houghton)
ABC Bunny by Wanda Gág (Coward)
Winged Girl of Knossos by Erik Berry (Appleton)
New Land by Sarah Schmidt (McBride)
Big Tree of Bunlahy: Stories of My Own Countryside by Padraic Colum (Macmillan)
Glory of the Seas by Agnes Hewes (Knopf)
Apprentice of Florence by Ann Kyle (Houghton)

1933
Winner:
Young Fu of the Upper Yangtze by Elizabeth Foreman Lewis (Winston)
Honor Books:
Swift Rivers by Cornelia Meigs (Little, Brown)
The Railroad to Freedom: A Story of the Civil War by Hildegarde Swift (Harcourt)
Children of the Soil: A Story of Scandinavia by Nora Burglon (Doubleday)

1932
Winner:
Waterless Mountain by Laura Adams Armer (Longmans)
Honor Books:
The Fairy Circus by Dorothy P. Lathrop (Macmillan)
Calico Bush by Rachel Field (Macmillan)
Boy of the South Seas by Eunice Tietjens (Coward-McCann)
Out of the Flame by Eloise Lownsbery (Longmans)
Jane's Island by Marjorie Allee (Houghton)
Truce of the Wolf and Other Tales of Old Italy by Mary Gould Davis (Harcourt)

1931
Winner:
The Cat Who Went to Heaven by Elizabeth Coatsworth (Macmillan)
Honor Books:
Floating Island by Anne Parrish (Harper)
The Dark Star of Itza: The Story of a Pagan Princess by Alida Malkus (Harcourt)
Queer Person by Ralph Hubbard (Doubleday)
Mountains Are Free by Julia Davis Adams (Dutton)
Spice and the Devil's Cave by Agnes Hewes (Knopf)
Meggy MacIntosh by Elizabeth Janet Gray (Doubleday)
Garram the Hunter: A Boy of the Hill Tribes by Herbert Best (Doubleday)
Ood-Le-Uk the Wanderer by Alice Lide and Margaret Johansen (Little, Brown)

1930
Winner:
Hitty, Her First Hundred Years by Rachel Field (Macmillan)
Honor Books:
A Daughter of the Seine: The Life of Madame Roland by Jeanette Eaton (Harper)
Pran of Albania by Elizabeth Miller (Doubleday)
Jumping-Off Place by Marion Hurd McNeely (Longmans)
The Tangle-Coated Horse and Other Tales by Ella Young (Longmans)
Vaino by Julia Davis Adams (Dutton)
Little Blacknose by Hildegarde Swift (Harcourt)

1929
Winner:
The Trumpeter of Krakow by Eric P. Kelly (Macmillan)
Honor Books:
Pigtail of Ah Lee Ben Loo by John Bennett (Longmans)
Millions of Cats by Wanda Gág (Coward)
The Boy Who Was by Grace Hallock (Dutton)
Clearing Weather by Cornelia Meigs (Little, Brown)
Runaway Papoose by Grace Moon (Doubleday)
Tod of the Fens by Elinor Whitney (Macmillan)

1928
Winner:
Gay-Neck, The Story of a Pigeon by Dhan Gopal Mukerji (Dutton)
Honor Books:
The Wonder Smith and His Son by Ella Young (Longmans)
Downright Dencey by Caroline Snedeker (Doubleday)

1927
Winner:
Smoky the Cowhorse by Will James (Scribner)

1926
Winner:
Shen of the Sea by Arthur Bowie Chrisman (Dutton)
Honor Book:
The Voyagers: Being Legends and Romances of Atlantic Discovery by Padraic Colum (Macmillan)

1925
Winner:
Tales from the Silver Lands by Charles Finger (Doubleday)
Honor Books:
Nicholas: A Manhattan Christmas Story by Annie Carroll Moore (Putnam)
The Dream Coach by Anne Parrish (Macmillan)

1924
Winner:
The Dark Frigate by Charles Boardman Hawes (Little, Brown)

1923
Winner:
The Voyages of Doctor Dolittle by Hugh Lofting (Lippincott)

1922
Winner:
The Story of Mankind by Hendrik Willem van Loon (Liveright)
Honor Books:
The Great Quest by Charles Hawes (Little, Brown)
Cedric the Forester by Bernard Marshall (Appleton)
The Old Tobacco Shop: A True Account of What Befell a Little Boy in Search of Adventure by William Bowen (Macmillan)
The Golden Fleece and the Heroes Who Lived Before Achilles by Padraic Colum (Macmillan)
The Windy Hill by Cornelia Meigs (Macmillan)